Common Management Challenges

and

How to Deal with Them

Common Management Challenges

and

How to Deal with Them

Ronald Hill, PhD

iUniverse, Inc.
Bloomington

COMMON MANAGEMENT CHALLENGES AND HOW TO DEAL WITH THEM

iUniverse books may be ordered through booksellers or by contacting:

iUniverse
1663 Liberty Drive
Bloomington, IN 47403
www.iuniverse.com
1-800-Authors (1-800-288-4677)

ISBN: 978-1-4759-8796-6 (sc)
ISBN: 978-1-4759-8797-3 (hc)
ISBN: 978-1-4759-8798-0 (e)

Library of Congress Catalog-in-Publication Data
Hill, Ronald
Common Management Challenges and How to Deal with
Them 1. Management. I. Hill, Ronald. II. Title
XXXX.XXXX 2013 xxxxx-xxxx
Library of Congress Control Number: 2013907567

Printed in the United States of America.

iUniverse rev. date: 6/4/2013

Contents

Preface: Staying Focused

In today's competitive business environment, there is limited time, resources, and energy to achieve results. On the flip side, there seemingly is no limit to the number of distractions facing today's manager. Staying focused on the vital few and not being distracted by the trivial many ensures maximum progress toward goals.

I have used the concept of *the vital few* throughout the book, breaking each common management challenge into three vital factors to be effectively dealt with. By focusing on the top three vital factors, it becomes much easier to stay focused on the vital aspects of managing and winning.

This publication is based on my personal management challenges encountered over thirty years, those challenges encountered while consulting with hundreds of managers at all corporate levels, and several years of reflection on actual management successes and failures and how to use this experience to enhance management performance.

Acknowledgments

This publication would not have been possible without all the people I have worked with during my academic and professional career. Their feedback relating to my performance, although not always what I wanted to hear, enabled me to reflect back on my career and how I could have significantly enhanced my personal performance above and beyond the success I did achieve. I share these lessons throughout this book.

My mentors during my career are too numerous to mention here, but I would especially like to thank the following people:

Bill Jensen, CEO of Intrawest, a leader in experiential destination resorts, who initially encouraged me to write this book and taught me to always go one step beyond just solving a problem.

Robert Bissell, former president of Wells Capital Management (a subsidiary of Wells Fargo), who over the years has been supportive of my ideas and demonstrates a human side of management to be admired.

Bud Runnels, one of my managers early on in my career, who taught me that my perception of my performance and capability doesn't always match others' perceptions and that providing honest, nonjudgmental feedback is critical to personal development.

Irving "Bud" Lyons, who allowed me the first opportunity to prove that my management theory works in a corporate-wide environment.

And last but not least, thanks to my wife, *Becky*, who kept the home fires burning while I chased my career all around the globe. She deserves more credit than I can ever give her.

Introduction

The idea for *Common Management Challenges and How to Deal with Them* has been in my mind for a number of years. For over thirty-five years, I was fortunate to have a career spanning positions from frontline worker bee to president and CEO of both public and private companies, as well as founding and successfully operating a management consulting business for twelve years. This has been complemented with nine years of undergraduate and graduate study, including a BS, MS, PhD, and MBA (all with high honors), and attendance at numerous management workshops and the reading of dozens of management-theory books.

During my career, I noticed that things tend to naturally fall into groups of three, as in these examples:

Forward, Neutral, Reverse	Red, White, Blue	Left, Right, Center
You, Me, Them	Morning, Noon, Night	Past, Present, Future
Father, Son, Holy Spirit	ABCs	Red, Yellow, Green (traffic light colors)
24, 7, 365	On Your Mark, Get Set, Go!	Ready, Aim, Fire!

When I retired, I took up the game of golf and soon realized it can be a very complex and frustrating sport. After trying to master everything—and failing—I decided to focus on just three basic things: grip, posture, and alignment. Once I mastered these three, I moved on to the next set of skills, and I found my game steadily improving.

Each day in my management career had many issues to be addressed, including numerous distractions defocusing my attention from what was really vital. Realizing that managing, like golf, can also be very complex and frustrating, it occurred to me that perhaps it would be possible to focus management functions into three basic concepts, forming a management foundation. When I applied this thinking to the general topic of management, I realized that management also has three key activities: planning, organizing, and implementing. Mastery of these basics provides a solid foundation for the mastery of other aspects of management. On the flip side, if you don't master these basics, your management career will be an exercise in frustration.

The lessons I learned during my professional career have all been invaluable and are based on real-life situations I had to face. In addition, during my management consulting years, I was able to witness and assess hundreds of managers at all levels of the corporate ladder. I realized that no matter their rank, managers can overlook opportunity, make fundamental mistakes, and quite often overlook their most important management tool: their staff.

It has been a lifelong journey of learning. The most important lesson I learned was the secret of how to succeed: namely, *stay focused on the vital few.* I have applied this lesson to the field of management and share these lessons in this publication. Each lesson focuses on three key elements necessary to effectively deal with common management challenges. It is my hope that these tips will provide you with an alternative to learning them the hard way.

Chapter 1

Count to Three and Succeed

Define Your Management Success.

Identify Critical Objectives.

Stay Focused on the Vital Few.

We can all count to three, and we can count a wide variety of different things, some of which may be critical to our success as managers and others that can be totally irrelevant. What we choose to count and focus on is the critical factor for achieving management success. Accidental success is as nice as it is rare. As the saying goes, "When you fail to plan, you plan to fail," and you are doomed to accept whatever happens.

Define Your Management Success.

Succeeding as a manager is a journey, and the odds for a successful journey increase dramatically when you plan. Like all journeys, the road to successful management begins with the first step: defining management success.

Early on in my career, I thought being successful meant doing a good job. I felt that promotions would come my way as long as I was producing results. Little did I realize this was only one part of the success formula. Being successful can mean several different things, such as getting a project done on time and within budget, meeting specs, building a team, delegating successfully, developing the team, developing yourself, or getting promoted, just to name a few.

While succeeding as a manager can include all of these factors, I realized that really succeeding as a manager was more encompassing than individual successes. So I set about defining management success. I reviewed dictionaries and searched the web for an encompassing definition of management success. I found it much easier to find a definition of the word *manage* than to find a definition of *management success.*

The verb *manage* can be defined as

> *to direct/oversee or control an enterprise, business, resource, expenditure, or people.*

Once this definition is understood, the extension to a more encompassing definition of *management success* is straightforward:

> *consistently directing/overseeing or controlling an enterprise, business, resource, expenditure, or people to achieve agreed-upon goals.*

If your performance matches this definition, you are successful as a manager, regardless of your position in your company. This is equally true whether you are the CEO or a frontline supervisor. However, achieving management success requires additional skill sets as one climbs the career ladder from supervisor to CEO, and these skill sets are vastly different at the CEO level from those at the supervisor level. And even though management success can occur at any management level, it is generally a prerequisite for advancement to the next management level. Thus, management success and career success are intimately intertwined.

Career success involves reaching a predefined goal that you have chosen. This can be any goal (such as being an individual contributor, achieving a specific management level, having the best team, consistently exceeding a plan, getting promoted, etc.), but defining that goal is absolutely critical to a successful career. Write this goal down and put it in a place you visit often, like your computer desktop. Make sure your goal is measurable and specific. Use the concept of SMART goals, that is, goals that are *specific, measurable, achievable, realistic, and time-limited.* Too many people fill their day with activities leading nowhere, and at the end of the day, they are one day older and no closer to achieving their goal. Sure, these activities may put bread on the table, ensure continued employment, and so on, and that is okay if this is your definition of career success. However, if you have more aggressive career ambitions, you undoubtedly have a specific position as your goal, which most likely includes being promoted to progressively responsible positions or changing jobs until you reach your ultimate goal.

Equally important to understanding management success is understanding your career goal and the stepping-stones leading to that goal. These stepping-stones are a series of intermediate, but critical, objectives that when successfully achieved will result in reaching your career goal.

Identify Critical Objectives.

In your quest to get promoted, equally important as being competent in your current position is getting ready to be competent at the next level. If you have defined promotions as part of your career success plan, the three critical objectives required to reach your goal are:

1. Learn the skills necessary to perform at the next level.

Although your first promotion was most likely due to the fact that you were good at your job, you rapidly discovered that being a good technician was totally different from managing a group of technicians. Before being promoted to the next level, learn the skills necessary to perform at the next level. Do this by observing or getting to know managers at the next level.

If possible, seek out a successful manager at that level who is willing to be your mentor. Ask him or her what it takes to succeed at that level. At least observe or talk to people who report to a successful manager at that level, and ask them their opinion of the skill set their manager possesses. At one point in my career, I needed to learn about manufacturing, so I asked a manufacturing manager if I could sit in on his management meetings to learn more about his operation. He was more than helpful and told me no one had ever approached him wanting to learn more about what he did.

2. Obtain the knowledge necessary to perform at the next level.

This can be done by asking people to recommend books to read, taking knowledgeable people to lunch and picking their brains (people love to talk about what they know), spending some time observing workers and how they do things, learning what management information systems managers at the next level use, and taking classes.

Oftentimes the next level requires some knowledge of a discipline other than the one you were trained in, such as moving from an engineering manager to a management position that includes overseeing manufacturing and accounting operations.

3. Promote yourself.

This simply means letting appropriate people know that you are interested in a position at the next level and asking them what you would need to do to be considered for promotion. Ask them if they would be willing to provide feedback as you acquire the necessary skills.

When I was in graduate school, I was finishing work on my master's thesis and looking for a project for my PhD. A friend of mine was in the final stages of research on his project, and there remained additional research to complete the total project. I approached his thesis advisor and asked if I could take over my friend's project when he graduated.

The advisor wasn't sure of my qualifications since my major had been electrical engineering and the project had to do with physics and metallurgy. I told him I had some knowledge of solid-state physics theory and asked what it would take to get the project's next phase for my research project. I also asked him what he would recommend I study in order to qualify. To make a long story short, I took his advice, and within three months, he gave me an oral exam and awarded me the project.

Stay Focused on the Vital Few.

Each day, review your activities and see if they have moved you closer to your objectives. Remember: those activities that move you closer to your goal are classified as vital, and vital activities that are most important at the current time are the vital few. There may be several vital activities at any point in time, not all of which can be done simultaneously. Pick the three most critical and get them done first. Don't move on to lesser objectives unless they can be worked on without delaying any of the three most critical objectives. Rigidly adhering to this discipline will guarantee the quickest path to success.

Be sure to differentiate between vital and urgent, as discussed in the next chapter.

Chapter 2

The Vital Few

Identify the Vital Few.

Don't Confuse Vital with Urgent.

Keep the Vital Factors Nonurgent.

Vilfredo Pareto, an Italian economist (1848–1923), is credited with the discovery of the 80-20 rule when he noticed that 80 percent of the wealth in Italy was controlled by just 20 percent of the population.[1]

Throughout time, others have made the same or similar observations. For example, Microsoft in 2003 noted that 80 percent of errors and crashes in Windows and Office were caused by 20 percent of the detected bugs.[2] Additionally, a 1992 United Nations Development Program Report showed that the richest 20 percent of the world's population controlled 82.7 percent of the world's income.[3]

Given that this appears to be the rule rather than the exception, the common extension of these observations states that 80 percent of results are obtained from 20 percent of the effort. Stated a different way, 20 percent of all activities produce 80 percent of the results. The activities that fall into this 20 percent category can be classified as the *vital few*.

What about the remaining 80 percent? How are they classified? Are they not important? While many activities contribute to successful goal attainment, the fact of the matter is that some contribute in a more significant manner than others. In other words, they are the most vital, while the remaining activities are *less* vital. These less vital activities, in relation to the vital activities yet to be performed, are referred to (in this book) as the *trivial many*. As time passes and the vital activities are completed, some of these trivial many will move into the vital few category, becoming the most important activities necessary for successful goal attainment.

Good managers have the ability to separate the vital from the trivial. Perhaps a bit overstated, the manager's golden rule should be "Concentrate on the vital few; ignore the trivial many." Sounds like good advice, but can a manager really ignore the trivial many? The answer is always yes if it impacts the ability to accomplish the vital few!

This is not to say that trivial activities should be tabled until the vital activities are completed. Obviously many activities get performed simultaneously with achieving business goals. The important lesson here is to make sure the vital few are being addressed to the greatest extent possible at all times and to not let the trivial few detract from that vital effort.

Identify the Vital Few.

The vital few can be time-dependent. For example, in project management there are usually several sequential and parallel activities leading to intermediate results (usually referred to as project milestones) that are vital to project completion. One can make the case that all these activities are vital, since eliminating any one of them results in incomplete goal attainment. However, at any given point in time, certain project activities are more vital than others, depending on whether or not delaying the activity delays project completion. These activities are referred to as *vital* and *urgent* and lie on the *critical path* (sequential activities that if delayed, delay goal attainment) and change with time as various activities are completed. At any given point in time, activities not on the critical path can take a certain amount of time longer than normal without impacting timely goal attainment (called slack time). However, as the activity consumes its slack time, it becomes part of the critical path and moves into the vital-urgent category. For a more complete discussion on project management theory, search the Internet for "project evaluation and review technique" (e.g., PERT) charts.

The vital few can also be time-independent if they are continually vital and urgent. Examples might be maintaining technical superiority in semiconductor products for a semiconductor manufacturer, maintaining product quality in any business, obtaining patent protection for products, maintaining long-term profitability, and so on.

Whether you are the CEO of a major corporation or manage a small group of individuals, you should identify and stay focused on the three most vital factors for success. Staying focused on three ensures that the top three priorities get accomplished first. Once one of the top three is accomplished, the next most important vital factor joins the top three. If there are more than three top priorities, the attention on each priority gets diluted.

Corporate executives for one company I consulted with had established fourteen corporate goals for the new year, all ranked as top corporate priorities. None of the managers I worked with could recite the top three goals, let alone all fourteen goals. By limiting priorities to the top three goals, the entire organization can understand and remember corporate priorities on a daily basis and make appropriate decisions on where to devote their effort.

Vital factors, whether urgent or not, need to be identified and tracked on a regular basis in order to ensure that they command the appropriate attention. Be careful to track the vital results you are looking for, in addition to the activities leading to the vital results.

For example, I was working with the manager of the loan officer group in a well-known bank whose goal was to produce new loans. At his weekly staff meeting, the loan officers were required to report new contacts made during the week. As a result, all the loan officers made sure they had contacts to report. However, the vital factor remained getting new loans, regardless of how many contacts were made. This tracking system placed the emphasis on activity instead of results. We changed the reporting procedure to include new loans closed as well as new contacts, quickly identifying loan officer productivity, allowing the team to set reasonable standards for loan generation, which in turn became the new criteria for acceptable performance.

In another example of the vital few, a manufacturer of stainless steel restaurant equipment (sinks, worktables, etc.) wanted to increase revenues and had identified that 30 percent of all proposals resulted in contracts. So the owner set goals for the sales force to increase the number of proposals generated. The number of submitted proposals met the new goals, but the sales remained the same. The owner was puzzled by this result. When we examined the newly generated proposals, we found that the sales force was meeting the new goals by splitting proposals into two or three separate proposals—one for sinks, one for tables, and so on. Once we explained the reasoning behind the new proposal goals (i.e., to increase sales, not just proposals) to the sales personnel, the sales force quit splitting the proposals and increased proposal activity, and the company began to realize its increased sales goal.

Don't Confuse Vital with Urgent.

Vital means the task is mission-critical, and *urgent* means the task needs to get done immediately or in the very near future. Just because something is urgent doesn't mean it is vital. For example, a task not on the critical path that is late, although vital, is not urgent until it becomes a task on the critical path.

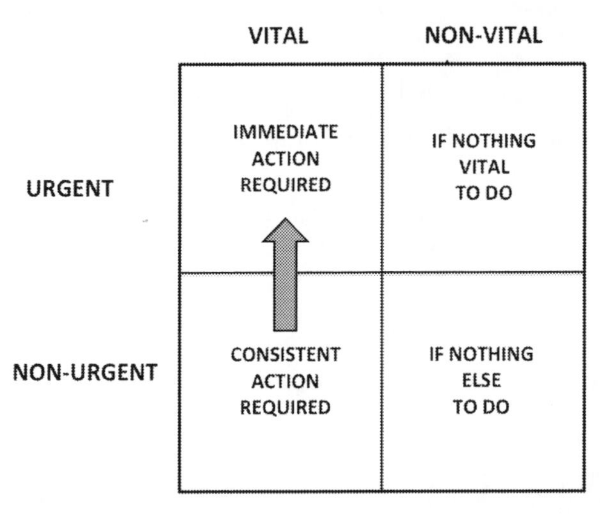

VITAL – URGENT MATRIX

Recognizing and addressing the vital few is the key to successful goal achievement. However, we are often distracted by non-vital tasks, especially if they are also urgent. The matrix above helps to stay focused on the vital factors.

Definitions:

Vital means it is mission-critical. In other words, if it is not completed, the mission will fail.

Non-vital is not mission-critical, and the mission can succeed without it.

Urgent means it is time-critical (i.e., it is approaching the deadline).

Nonurgent means there is still adequate time to complete it.

If something is vital and also urgent, it must be addressed immediately to keep the project on track. You have no choice because if an item is not addressed immediately, the project will not be completed as scheduled. If it is vital but nonurgent, it is no less critical, but there is still time to complete it without delaying the project. However, if not completed, as the arrow indicates, it will migrate from vital-nonurgent to vital-urgent.

If it is urgent but non-vital, it should be addressed only after vital items that can be currently addressed have been addressed. An example of this might be a deadline to renew a magazine subscription.

Non-vital and nonurgent are don't-care items to be addressed only if there is nothing else to do.

Keep the Vital Factors Nonurgent.

In the beginning, the vital items are usually nonurgent, since there is still time left before the vital task has to be completed.

As time passes, the vital become more and more urgent, usually because the trivial many detract from the vital few. The manager who spends too much time on the non-vital issues will find the vital issues migrating from the vital-nonurgent to the vital and urgent arena. When this happens, there often isn't enough time to adequately accomplish the vital tasks, resulting in delays and cost overruns.

The trick is to continually address the vital items while they are still nonurgent. This requires regular action or activity to keep the vital-nonurgent moving forward toward completion. This is accomplished by tracking the vital-nonurgent right after you finish tracking the vital-urgent factors. This regular monitoring will keep attention on these vital factors while they are still nonurgent. The tracking priority for any project should be to first track the vital-urgent; second, track the vital-nonurgent; and third, track the urgent-non-vital.

Chapter 3

The Ideal Manager

THE SMART – DUMB MANAGER MATRIX

	SMART	DUMB
AMBITIOUS		
LAZY		

I was having lunch with one of my clients in Stuttgart, Germany, and we were discussing various management styles. I was asked, "What are the characteristics of the most effective manager?" After a brief discussion, my client further asked, "If you had your choice, would you choose a manager who was smart and ambitious, smart and lazy, dumb and ambitious, or dumb and lazy?" I remember thinking what an easy choice this was, and immediately chose *smart and ambitious*. The ensuing discussion is a lesson I have always remembered.

We both agreed we could rule out *dumb and lazy* immediately since these managers are too dumb to know what to do, and even if they did know what to do, they would be too lazy to do it.

Likewise, after some discussion, we both agreed that the *dumb and ambitious* managers can be ruled out because they are too dumb to know if what they are doing is effective or not but are so ambitions that they set off doing things, most likely the wrong things.

My choice, the *smart and ambitious* manager, appeared to me to be the likely choice, but my client pointed out that these managers are smart enough to know what to do, but being ambitious, they roll up their sleeves and start doing it and soon get so busy they can't accomplish any additional tasks. This can happen at the highest levels of management. One of my consulting assignments was coaching a senior VP who was failing in his job. He was responsible for $750 million in annual revenues, and although he had a staff of five very capable people, he retained all major responsibilities for himself. Is it any wonder he was not succeeding?

This leaves the *smart and lazy* manager. "How does a lazy manager get anything done?" I asked. "Ah-ha!" my client responded. "The smart and lazy manager is only lazy when it involves doing tasks that other members of the team are capable of performing. Being smart, these managers rapidly figure out that they can get others to do the tasks, enabling the accomplishment of more than they could ever do alone. In other words, they delegate!"

In retrospect, this principle is fairly obvious, but by the up-and-coming manager, the concept is often overlooked while the very capable performer is busy doing what others could be doing. Similar to the concept of using financial leverage to increase return on your investment, delegation is leveraging your labor by using others to increase results.

No matter how talented a person is or how much stamina or dedication a person has, there is always a limit to how much he or she can personally accomplish in a given period of time. Granted, some people are personally capable of achieving spectacular results, but they are still limited by the ticking of the clock. By investing their time in properly delegating to other team members, the amount of time spent simultaneously achieving results increases with each delegated task, resulting in several top performers achieving results simultaneously.

A cardinal rule for managers to observe at all times to achieve maximum results is to make sure their team is fully engaged in productive activity before taking on tasks personally. Only when the team is fully engaged will the manager's personal efforts effectively contribute to the outcome.

A common crutch used by managers who limit delegation or don't delegate is "I can do it faster myself." This is probably true, but how many things can these managers simultaneously do faster themselves? In the long run, these managers will run out of time or results will deteriorate. Rather than personally taking on additional tasks, these managers are much better off investing their time in teaching others how to do the job in an acceptable manner. I call this "leveraging management time."

Levers allow the lifting of more weight than possible without the lever, and in a similar manner, when managers teach and delegate, they are creating the capacity to accomplish more than they can individually accomplish.

Chapter 4

The Management Danger Zone

You Get Promoted.

You Encounter the Performance Gap.

You Fall into the Performance Trap.

The management danger zone occurs when managers have so many tasks to do that they don't have enough time in a day to accomplish them (or they have to work ten to twelve hours per day just to keep up). There is a sequence of events that can easily place a manager in this so-called danger zone, resulting in high levels of stress, less personal time, less family time, less time for maintaining health, and so on.

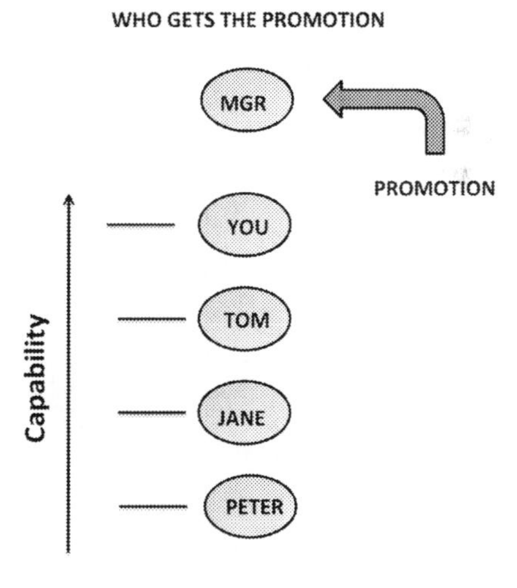

You Get Promoted.

It all begins with being promoted.

You are probably very capable in your job, probably the most capable or one of the most capable people doing your specific job. Thus, because of your expertise, you are promoted to a management position (or the next level of management). This usually occurs with little or no management training. Somehow you are expected to know how to manage others as effectively as you performed your previous job.

As the newly promoted manager, you will most likely be spending part of your time performing some technical work, as well as spending some time attending to your management duties. As you continue to move up the corporate ladder, you ideally should be spending more and more management time on management activities and less and less time on technical work.

Management vs. Technical Work

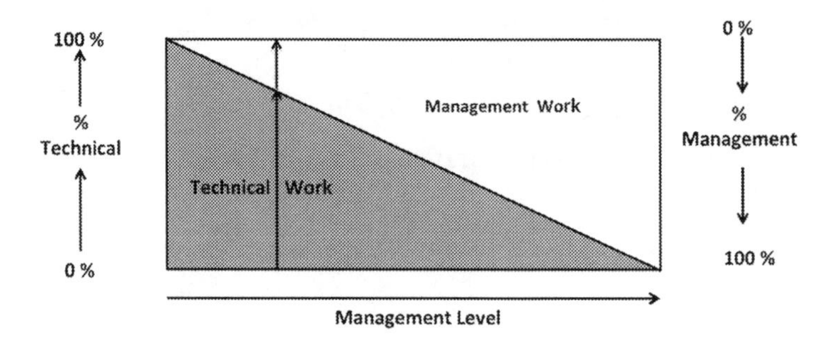

You Encounter the Performance Gap.

Since you were one of the best at your previous job, you are now managing personnel performing tasks similar to your previous job. And, of course, you want the tasks performed as well as you were capable of performing them. But the personnel you were promoted over aren't quite as good as you were, so you get frustrated with the results. As a result, you are reluctant to delegate.

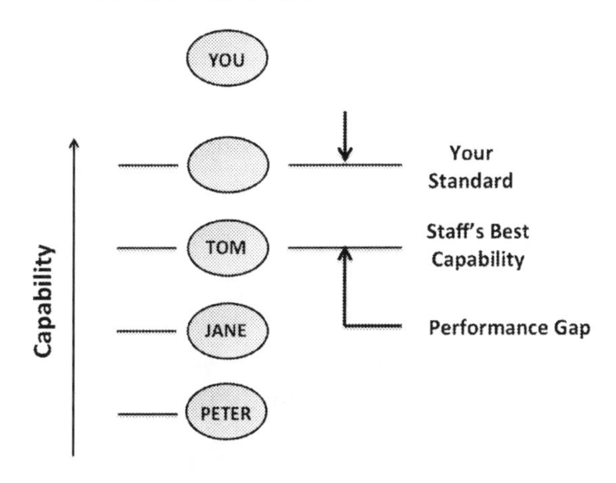

You Fall into the Performance Trap.

So you lend a helping hand, especially in a time crunch, when you fall into the mode of "I'll do it myself just this once" to get it done on time as well as it can be done.

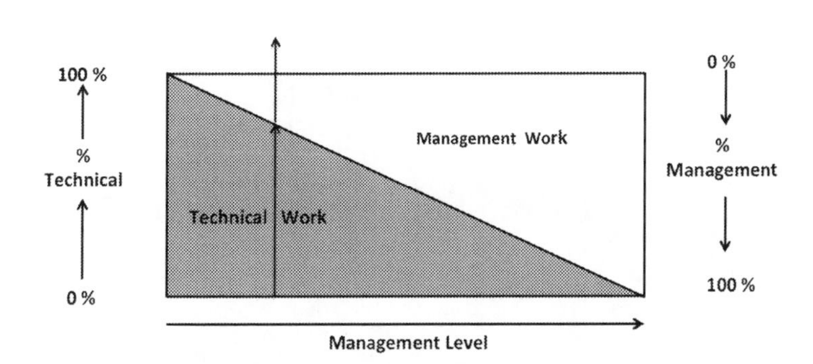

But of course, "just this once" turns into "just one more time" and by your stepping in, your organization (with your contributions) excels.

The Second Performance Trap

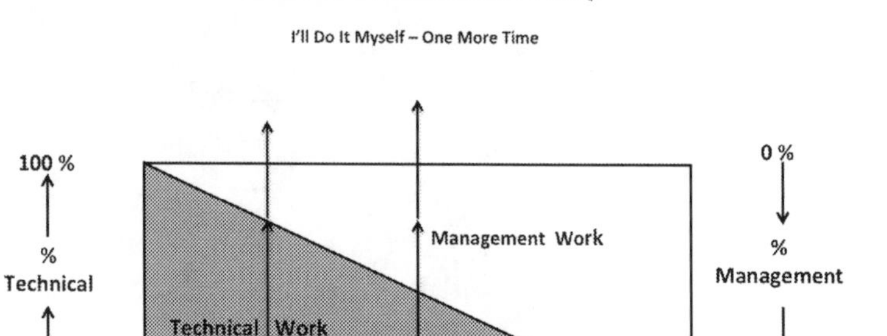

So you are again promoted, and the pattern repeats itself until, at some point, you are totally maxed out and begin to falter. Your family is being neglected, your health begins to suffer, and because results are now slipping, you work even harder to compensate. Guess what! You are now firmly entrenched in the danger zone.

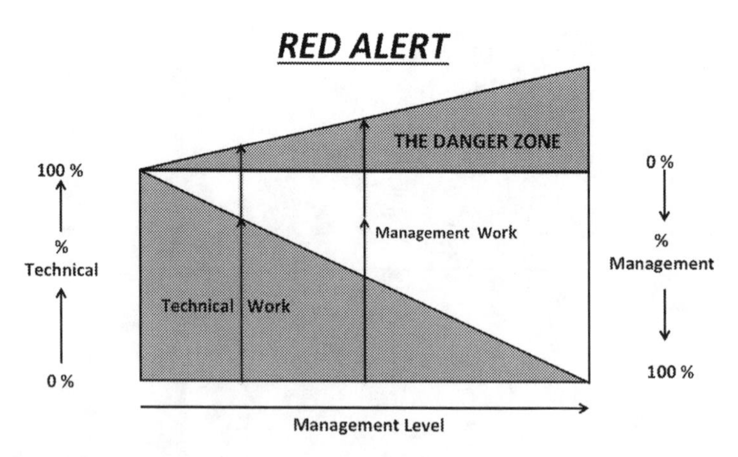

The obvious answer here is to delegate effectively. If your staff is not as capable as you, help them learn; assist them in getting the task done instead of doing it yourself. Make sure you are training and developing your staff's capability and expertise to produce acceptable results.

To determine if you are a danger-zone candidate, make a list of all the tasks you perform, and then identify the tasks that *only you* can perform. The difference tells you how far into the danger zone you are.

Chapter 5

Avoiding the Danger Zone

Do.

Delegate.

Dump.

What to do, who should do it, and should it be done are common management questions. The ability to sort through this maze is essential if one is to succeed as a manager. Your team is depending on you to organize and lead the team, which becomes impossible if most of the time you are all tangled up trying to decide what to do or who should be doing it. In addition, your management is depending on you to get things done on time and within budget. Once again, that is nearly impossible if you are all tangled up trying to decide what to do or who should be doing it.

Oftentimes, as people evolve into being managers (often with no management training), they haven't thought about who should be doing what, let alone what they should be doing themselves. Developing criteria to deal with these questions greatly simplifies a manager's life on a daily basis. There are certain things managers can do and should do, as well as things managers can do but should delegate rather than do themselves.

Do.

As a manager, there are certain things that cannot be delegated, which you must personally do. Managers often find themselves overwhelmed with tasks and never stop to consider if they personally have to be doing them.

One of my favorite exercises in management workshops I facilitate is to ask the participants to jot down all the tasks they are currently performing and then circle those items that only they can do. I then ask all the participants to reveal the number of tasks they are performing and then reveal the number of tasks that only they can do. I have never had a workshop where a participant was the only one who could do all the tasks on his or her initial list.

Try this exercise yourself and see if you are delegating effectively. If you find yourself saying "But I don't have anyone qualified to do the task," you are simply identifying the need to get your staff trained, perhaps by assisting them in accomplishing the task until they are qualified or else arranging appropriate staff training.

Delegate.

Having identified a task that can be delegated, the next step is to identify the person who should perform the task. The person responsible for the task may not be fully capable of performing the task, so you may be tempted to delegate to a more capable person. If you choose that person, you are probably overloading that individual and delegating a task he or she knows someone else should be doing, leading to frustration for that employee (i.e., "It seems the more I do, the more I get assigned to do").

If the person who should be performing the delegated task isn't fully capable of performing the task satisfactorily, work with that employee until he or she can do it satisfactorily or provide the necessary training for him or her to obtain the necessary skill.

To allow team members to assume ownership and enhance probability for successful completion when you delegate, delegate in terms of expected results, not how to do the task. This allows team members to use their creativity and possibly succeed beyond your expectations. As the general manager of a division with profit and loss responsibility, I suspected accounting was erroneously charging my division with expenses belonging to other divisions. Instead of tracking and verifying this key item myself, I delegated the task to my administrative assistant by asking her to make sure expenses charged to our cost center were valid expenses. She, in turn, worked out a monthly system with accounting to verify expenses, and at the end of the year, she had reversed over $60,000 in erroneous expenses charged to our division.

When you tell someone how to do the job, you don't transfer ownership for results; the ownership remains with you, not with the person you delegated to.

Dump.

Stay focused on the vital few to achieve maximum results. Remember: 80 percent of the results come from 20 percent of the effort. Periodically evaluate the tasks you are personally performing, and if they are not management tasks you should be performing to effectively engage your team's efforts, consider dumping them. If you find yourself in a hole, quit digging.

Additionally, it is a good idea to periodically review tasks being performed by members of your team, and dump those tasks not contributing to team goals. I have oftentimes found team members performing tasks they thought I wanted done even though I had never asked them to perform these tasks. (See chapter 38, "Communications Advice," and chapter 39, "Effective Communication Factors.") Reflecting back on those situations, I have to take responsibility either for not clearly communicating goals and vital factors for achieving goals or not effectively monitoring staff activities.

Finally, make sure your staff understands the difference between vital and non-vital, as well as urgent and nonurgent.

Chapter 6

Keys to Effective Delegation

Pick the Right Person.

Delegate Expected Results, Not How-To.

Set Up Tracking Mechanisms.

As the manager, it's easy to assign tasks to others. But effective delegation is more than just assigning tasks. Oftentimes a manager may be dumping tasks on team members instead of delegating them.

Pick the Right Person.

Make sure the person you are delegating to can accomplish the delegated task. As an electrical engineering student working part-time for an aerospace company, I was assigned the task of designing a cooling exhaust vent for a rack of electronic equipment. I had no idea how to proceed or any knowledge of mechanical tooling or processes that I could employ. I relayed this concern to my supervisor but was told to give it a try anyway. In short, the task was dumped on me. Needless to say, the box I designed was tossed out at the first review, and the task was reassigned to a mechanical engineer.

Match the person to the results expected. Make sure the chosen person has the skills to accomplish what you are asking. Then make sure that what you are delegating is reasonable and can be accomplished in the specified time frame and that the person you are delegating to has the tools and support to do the job.

Delegate Expected Results, Not How-To.

Transfer ownership by letting (within reason) the person delegated to determine how to accomplish the desired results. You may know a way to accomplish the goal, but the person you are delegating to may have a better, more efficient way of accomplishing the same result. It's okay to discuss his or her plan as a reality check and ask questions, but if you can see that this plan will achieve the desired results, get out of the way and let him or her go. Don't be a wing-clipper. When you specify how to get the job done, it becomes your plan, not your employee's. The employee's effort to successfully accomplish his or her plan will always outweigh his or her effort to accomplish your plan.

Set Up Tracking Mechanisms.

When you delegate, establish a tracking mechanism consistent with the time frame required to accomplish the delegated tasks. The onus to report progress should be on the people you delegate to, so you don't have to babysit their progress. For example, you can simply request a status report once a week at a specified time. If they miss the status report, remind them of it ("I guess I must not have made myself clear on status reports, so let's review them now" is a nice way of reminding without blaming). Without this tracking mechanism, you have simply abdicated, and you will get whatever the results are with little ability to affect the outcome.

Use common sense when setting up the tracking system. If it is a monthlong task, you might ask to be updated once a week at a specific time (that way you can schedule the update on your calendar); but if it is a task scheduled for two days, you might only track it when due to be completed.

Having set up tracking mechanisms with your staff, make sure you schedule time to track progress as scheduled with your staff. Failure to do this will communicate that adhering to the tracking schedule isn't all that important.

Chapter 7

The Monkey Mirror

The Monkey Appears.

The Monkey Mirror Reflects the Monkey.

The Monkey Disappears.

The expression "I've got a monkey on my back" commonly refers to an unsolved problem a person is dealing with. Managers have no shortage of monkeys during their career. Some of these monkeys legitimately belong to the manager, for example: overdue performance reviews, being over budget, project delays, and so on. However, monkeys that have found a comfortable home on a manager's back often belong to someone else.

The Monkey Appears.

With plenty of legitimate monkeys, why would a manager accept others' monkeys? Obviously no one wants to accept another person's problems, but this happens all the time, often with the manager's best intentions. In some cases, managers may not be comfortable delegating tasks, for a variety of reasons: they are not comfortable with a team member's abilities, time is short so they take on tasks themselves, team members are already overloaded, and so on. In this case, the monkey stays with the manager and never makes it to the team member's back. This reluctance takes the manager into the danger zone (see chapter

4, "The Management Danger Zone," and chapter 5, "Avoiding the Danger Zone").

In other cases, team members with a monkey on their back often approach the manager seeking help with their monkey (i.e., problem), hoping to transfer the monkey to the manager's back. The manager may be busy when approached or may not have a ready solution to offer and so tells the team members that he or she will have to get back to them. When this happens, the monkey has just leaped from the team member's back to the manager's back. The team member has been relieved of responsibility for the problem until the manager gets back to him or her, which may take some time or may never happen.

The Monkey Mirror Reflects the Monkey.

Managers can significantly reduce the number of monkeys leaping onto their backs in this manner by using the monkey mirror to reflect the monkey back to the team member.

The monkey-mirror conversation goes like this:

Team Member:	"Can you help me with a problem?"
Manager:	"What's the problem?"
Team Member:	Explains the problem.
Manager:	Uses the monkey mirror by saying, "What do you think you should do to resolve this problem?"

Team Member: Uses the *anti-monkey-mirror defense* by saying, "I don't know. That's why I'm asking you."

Manager: Uses the *anti-anti-monkey-mirror response* by saying, "Think of three things you could do to resolve this problem and get back to me."

The Monkey Disappears.

At this point, the team member has little recourse but to think of three things that might resolve the problem.

Team Member: "The three things I might do are …" (Team Member lists three things.)

Manager: "Which one do you think is the best solution?"

Team Member: States his or her choice.

Manager: "Great. Go ahead and implement your solution."

The monkey has been successfully reflected to its rightful owner.

Chapter 8

Key Management Tasks

Establish Goals.

Develop and Implement Plans.

Support Your Staff.

As a manager in today's hectic environment, it is easy to get focused on solving problems and get distracted from the fundamental management tasks of establishing goals, developing and implementing plans to accomplish these goals, and finally, supporting those who will make it happen, your staff.

Establish Goals.

It all begins with the end in sight: establishing goals for your team. There are two types of goals that are needed in any successful organization. The first type is essential for successfully performing your job (and keeping your job), and the second type is characteristic of the smart manager, who succeeds over the long term. The first type is to get the job done. You and your organization are charged with producing certain results on an ongoing basis, for example: meet sales quota, achieve specified gross margins, and so on. The second type is to set goals to improve team performance beyond current levels. These goals ensure continual improvement, essential in today's business environment. With these two types of goals in place, the smart manager is getting the daily job done while simultaneously improving the team's capability for enhanced future performance.

This dual-goal concept was evident in a printer company I consulted with: the first goal was to produce a printer at a competitive price in a given amount of time, and the second goal was to reduce the manufacturing cost by 50 percent every two years. For the engineers striving to meet the first goal, the second goal seemed well out of reach, and some engineers stressed out over the second goal while still trying to meet the first goal. The successful engineers focused on meeting the first goal, albeit keeping the second goal in mind, and were able to meet the cost and schedule targets. Then they focused on the second goal, to reduce the manufacturing cost during the next two years, and in fact, were able to achieve it.

Develop and Implement Plans.

A goal without a plan to achieve it is wishful thinking, with very little likelihood of success. Plans include sequential and parallel (simultaneous) tasks leading to goal achievement, as well as personnel with identified responsibilities for performing these tasks within specified time frames.

However, the fact that a plan and responsibility have been established doesn't guarantee success. In fact, almost all projects don't proceed according to the original plan, and responsibilities have a habit of being modified or changed completely during the course of the project. Murphy's law is always in play, and if something can go wrong, it will! Thus, it is necessary to track progress toward goals on a regular basis to identify deviation from the plan and to take corrective action to keep the goal on target.

It is a rare project that goes according to plan, so recognize that being off of plan and taking corrective action is the norm. Use the PGA (Problem–Goal–Action) process to accomplish this (see chapter 17 for details).

Support Your Staff.

During the course of implementation, the most important role a manager plays is to make sure the team has everything needed to succeed. No matter how talented a manager is, there is a finite limit as to how much he or she can accomplish as an individual. Personal accomplishments are important if you are an individual contributor, but as a manager, you will be judged on how well your organization achieves goals. Thus, you are dependent on your staff to ensure your success as a manager. With this understood, supporting your staff in their efforts to achieve their individual (and coordinated) goals is tantamount to supporting yourself in achieving your organizational and career goals.

Chapter 9

Plan, Organize, Implement

The Planning Phase.

The Organizing Phase.

The Implementation Phase.

Three key elements of managing are: planning, selecting a strategy, and implementing that plan. Each phase has different characteristics and criteria.

The Planning Phase.

Planning is the process of knowing where you're at (situation analysis), where you want to be (goal), and how you're going to get there (strategy). To facilitate obtaining the best plans, this phase must be open to inputs and be nonjudgmental. Discussion is the dominant process: considering alternatives, impacts, feasibility, and so on. The end result is to have the goal clearly defined, with alternative ways of achieving the goal.

There are generally a variety of ways to achieve any given goal. These various ways, called strategies, usually require different action plans to achieve the goal. For example, the goal may be to increase profitability, and various strategies might include: expense reduction, increased revenue, sale of assets, merger or acquisition, and so on. Obviously, these paths to increased profitability differ widely. However, one path must be chosen as the strategy to achieve the goal, along with the corresponding action plans. Factors affecting the choice usually include many considerations, such as feasibility, cost, resource availability, staff expertise, competition, vendor reliability, and so on.

The Organizing Phase.

Organizing means lining up the resources necessary to accomplish the goal. This includes finalizing plans and strategies, communicating them, identifying personnel and their responsibilities, establishing time frames, establishing mileposts, obtaining necessary materials and equipment, and setting up tracking procedures.

The Implementation Phase.

Once the alternative plans have been considered and strategies have been chosen to achieve goals, it's time to implement. While the planning and strategy selection phases are characterized by lots of discussion, the implementation phase is action-oriented. Alternatives have already been discussed and chosen or eliminated. Second-guessing is a waste of time. If the strategy is failing, implement contingency plans expeditiously.

Personnel involved in hazardous professions spend a lot of time planning and training before their skills are put to the test. Firefighters are a good example of this. They have usually already determined the best actions to take for most emergency situations and rely on their training, rather than inventing solutions during the emergency. While the manager's role may not be hazardous, nevertheless, implementing the plan rather than developing the plan as you go along is key.

Chapter 10

Identifying Strengths, Weaknesses, Opportunities, and Threats (SWOT Charts)

Identify Strengths and Weaknesses.

Take Advantage of Opportunities.

Eliminate or Mitigate Threats.

SWOT is an acronym for strengths, weaknesses, opportunities, and threats. Making a chart of these four factors is a useful planning tool to focus on strengths to overcome weaknesses, take advantage of opportunities, and mitigate threats. The idea here is to use team brainstorming to identify as many factors in each category as possible. Once identified, prioritize the various factors and make sure your team is dealing with at least the top three factors in each category, using strengths to overcome weaknesses, realize opportunities, and eliminate threats.

S.W.O.T CHART EXAMPLE

STRENGTHS	**WEAKNESSES**
Market Recognition	Technical Expertise
OPPORTUNITIES	**THREATS**
Train Staff Redesign Products	Product Obsolescence

Identify Strengths and Weaknesses.

A primary use of the SWOT chart in your planning process is to use brainstorming to identify the team's strengths and weaknesses. Lack of a strength can be considered a weakness if it is necessary to achieve goals just as a lack of weakness can be considered a strength. By having the team fill in the SWOT chart strengths and weaknesses on one chart, the holes (lack of strengths) can be easily identified as well as apparent weaknesses. Priorities and goals can then be established to plug holes in strengths and eliminate weaknesses.

Take Advantage of Opportunities.

The SWOT brainstorming process helps ensure that hidden opportunities emerge. Different team members will see the same as well as different opportunities, ensuring that as many opportunities as possible are identified. By prioritizing these opportunities the team can establish goals that will provide maximum benefits.

Eliminate or Mitigate Threats.

Once again, the brainstorming process used in developing the SWOT chart helps identify actual or potential threats, including threats that may not be immediately obvious. Once identified, the team can determine which threats need to be eliminated, which threats only need to be mitigated, and which threats can be ignored (if any).

Chapter 11

Three Types of Information

Latent.

Current.

Predictive.

Information is the key to survival in today's business environment regardless of whether you are in the private or public sector. Consider the following three types of information when setting up your information systems.

Latent.

Latent information is information about what has already happened. Its value lies in the revelation of what has been achieved in the past, what caused it to happen, what effects it had on our environments, what impact it had on our success or failure, and so on. In essence, latent information is a learning tool, that is, we learn from past mistakes and successes.

Current.

Current information is information about what is happening now and is valuable in making informed and accurate corrective action decisions to stay on plan or take advantage of unexpected opportunity. This type of information is not as easily obtained as latent information, so care needs to be taken in designing your information system to separate fact from rumor and provide you with correct and vital current information.

Routine information, such as being on plan (while necessary), shouldn't bury vital information, such as early detection of deviations from plan. Anything that affects the ability to achieve vital goals needs to be elevated in visibility above routine information. Validate information sources, eliminate unreliable sources, and determine and keep those sources that provide accurate, consistent, and timely information.

Predictive.

Good predictive information can go a long way toward achieving success, but on the flip side, bad predictive information can lead to disastrous results. The old saying "GIGO" (Garbage In, Garbage Out) is very apropos for developing predictive information. Make sure you have accurate data feeding your forecasting models. Look for trends in such data at daily, weekly, or monthly checkpoints, and especially in YTD (year-to-date) projections. Use good statistical tools to develop your predictive data, but always remember the future is not always predictable, so keep a close eye on activities based on predictive data.

The old saying "If you continue to do what you've always done, you will continue to get what you've always got" is as true today as it was yesterday and as true as it will be tomorrow. This is the basis for the power of using year-to-date (YTD) projections to predict the future. It is not unusual for daily operations to continue day after day, week after week, with little or no change in procedures or methodology. When this is the case, the future is fairly predictable by extending historical results (trends) into the future, providing valuable information upon which to base future decisions such as revenue, expenses, and so on.

I was consulting with a real estate company during a fairly stable period in the economy, and the owners were considering revenues and expenses for the second half of their fiscal year. One of the owners was very optimistic about increased future revenues. Knowing that their plan did not include any substantial changes from past operations and economic forecasts predicted similar conditions for the remainder of the year, I performed a "least squares best-fit analysis" on the available YTD data for the last year, and I projected the results to forecast revenues for the remainder of the fiscal year.

My results disagreed with the partner's beliefs, and he bet me a case of fine wine that his projections would be met. I was so confident in my results that I accepted his bet on the condition that he would not have to pay up if he lost but I would buy him the wine of his choice if I lost the bet. As it turned out, my forecast was right on the money and fell considerably short of his *hopium* forecast. Of course, had the economy changed dramatically or the owners changed their operations in a significant manner, I would have had to revisit my forecast.

The lesson here is that if you are predicting significant changes in future results, you had better be able to identify the cause for the change. The housing market behavior during the period 2000 to 2008 should have been predictable. As credit requirements were significantly lowered with below-prime ARMs (Adjustable Rate Mortgages), the market was bound to heat up, as more and more would-be buyers were able to afford the lower monthly payments. However, this bubble was bound to burst when it came time to refinance the ARMs (which were at all-time low-interest rates). When interest rates increased and homeowners found themselves unable to afford the new monthly mortgage payments, the bubble burst quickly and violently. This in turn glutted the market with people trying to sell their homes or finding their homes going into foreclosure.

Of course, hindsight is 20-20, but one cannot help wondering why someone didn't ask, "What if interest rates increase? What if the sales inventory skyrockets?"

Chapter 12

Performance Levels

Adequate Performance.

Good Performance.

Excellent Performance.

Performance comes in many flavors, ranging from unacceptable to it-doesn't-get-any-better. As a manager, one of your primary responsibilities is to move personnel from adequate to excellent performance. To do this, you need to understand the basis for the three performance levels and what to do about it.

Adequate Performance.

Adequate performance gets the job done, but is just a notch above marginal performance. Adequate performance is minimally acceptable. If performance in your organization is ranked, *adequate* should be at the bottom of the scale. While you may not get fired for your team's adequate performance, you may be one of the first to go during layoffs. The manager's job, among other things, is to provide motivation, tools, training, and opportunity to gain experience, and to minimize uncontrollable factors. Not meeting these requirements guarantees continued mediocrity.

Adequate performance can be the result of many factors: lack of pride in one's work, inadequate tools, inadequate training, inadequate experience, or factors beyond one's control. However, successful managers always strive to find ways over, around, under, or through these obstacles and achieve more than adequate team performance.

Good Performance.

Good performance exceeds minimum acceptable levels but still has room for improvement. Good managers make sure they recognize and reward good performance, while encouraging and challenging personnel to achieve continually improving performance.

From a team perspective, this may require aligning personnel talents to match task requirements, establishing peer mentoring programs, and so forth. It will also require honest performance appraisals, giving credit where credit is due, pointing out opportunity for improvement, and allowing staff to establish their own action plans to achieve higher performance levels. Ask staff members what they believe they are capable of and what they need from you to achieve higher performance. And when they achieve higher performance levels, make sure you let them know that you are aware of their successes.

Nothing is more demotivating than exerting effort to increase personal performance and having it go unrecognized by management. Be a recognizer, not an ignorer.

Excellent Performance.

Excellent performance is at the top of the scale, but performance won't stay excellent without proper maintenance. This will include previously mentioned factors, such as ongoing training, recognition, and so on. It also includes continual awareness of and adoption of changing factors, such as new or emerging technologies, keeping track of competition, fostering creative thinking, being open to new ways of thinking, encouraging experimentation with new or different ways of getting the job done, and so on.

Make sure you are an enabling manager and not an inhibiting manager. Look for ways to enable personnel. Recognize that people would rather be top performers than mediocre performers. Good managers recognize that maintaining excellent performance involves incorporating new ways of doing things. As new concepts are incorporated, a good manager understands that the team's experience and therefore performance with a new concept will move from adequate to good to excellent as each new concept is incorporated. A good manager provides necessary encouragement during this transition.

Chapter 13

Effective Performance Reviews

Establish Performance Standards.

Be Honest.

Provide Feedback.

One of a manager's most effective tools for improving or achieving desired performance is the performance review. Oftentimes, due to demands on a manager's time, these reviews are no more than a pat on the back and an annual pay raise. By taking the time to give effective performance reviews, you greatly enhance your team's ability to perform at higher levels.

Establish Performance Standards.

In order to effectively review an individual's performance, performance standards need to be established. In a goal-oriented organization, this is somewhat easier, since individuals have specific goals regarding quantity, quality, cost, and time.

Without goals, performance becomes subjective rather than objective. Consider, for example, the statement "Does a good job" (highly subjective) versus "Consistently meets goals" (measurable and quantifiable). Which one is more meaningful? Standards allow one to quantify performance. For example, superior performance might mean meeting goals at least 95 percent of the time; excellent, 85 to 95 percent; good, 75 to 85 percent; and inadequate, less than 75 percent.

In addition to specific individual goals, set standards for things like teamwork, positive attitude, honesty, employee development, and so on. While this may seem subjective, it can be accomplished by providing an anonymous 360 review (a candid review provided by people an employee works with answering questions such as, What percent of the time does this person demonstrate a positive attitude? What percent of the time does this person demonstrate a commitment to teamwork? What percent of the time does this person demonstrate honesty?). It is then a simple manner to assign break points in these ratings, such as superior, excellent, good, and so on, as described above. The 360 review is usually accomplished with the aid of a neutral third party such as a personal or management consultant who can compile feedback while offering anonymity to people providing feedback. The anonymity factor helps ensure candor in the feedback.

Be Honest.

The biggest disservice managers can provide an employee is to not be honest about their view of the employee's performance. Honest feedback enables an employee to focus on improvement, or at least correct what the employee perceives to be an inaccurate assessment. At a bare minimum, honest feedback provides the opportunity for the employee and manager to resolve differences of opinion regarding performance.

At one point in my career, I reported to a manager responsible for a product line completely different from my product line. He knew very little about my product line and felt I should be reporting to his manager instead of him and wanted to promote me to his peer level. However, his manager wouldn't agree, so I asked the reluctant manager for an audience and asked him why. He told me candidly that he didn't know if I were capable and didn't know if he could trust me. I suggested I report to him temporarily for three months, and if I couldn't overcome his objection, he could demote me, no questions asked. Needless to say, I was so motivated to prove him wrong, the promotion only took one month.

This manager could have avoided a truthful assessment by offering innumerable excuses, such as, "The budget won't permit me to promote you," "I don't have the time to supervise another person," "My manager won't approve," and so on. When he gave me an honest answer, I was able to realize how he perceived me and overcome his concerns. Had he hidden behind lame excuses, neither of us would have benefited.

Provide Feedback.

Performance reviews should not be limited to an annual event associated with a salary review. Too often, being associated with a salary review diminishes the importance of the performance feedback. Quarterly performance reviews can be more effective and provide the employee four opportunities per year to align performance expectations. And if salary reviews are an annual event, the performance review at the annual event shouldn't be a surprise.

Feedback is a two-way street. In addition to providing feedback, ask for feedback about your performance. How does the team member view your performance as a manager? However, be careful how you ask for feedback. Don't put your team member on the spot by asking him or her to criticize your performance. Rather, ask if there are things you could be doing to make his or her job easier or more efficient, to remove roadblocks, and so on. Never fall into the trap of believing lack of success is always others' fault. Be willing and open to receiving feedback.

Chapter 14

Correcting Poor Performance

Identify the Performance Issue.

Identify Reasons for the Shortfall.

Determine Corrective Actions.

When I consider my role as a manager, I often visualize myself as an old country doctor with a little black bag taken to all house calls. That bag contained all kinds of medical magic, ranging from pills to hypodermics, from thermometers to Band-Aids, and a variety of other tools. At the bottom of the doctor's little black bag was a small saw, in case all the other tools proved ineffective and amputation was the last resort. The doctor would inevitably try other remedies before resorting to the saw, for once the saw was used, the other contents in the bag were of little use.

My little black management bag is very similar to that doctor's medicine bag. I have lots of management tools inside, such as rewarding results, giving honest, effective performance reviews, taking corrective action, and so on. I always start off by using a variety of these tools, but in the back of my mind, like the doctor's saw, I know I have a hammer in the bottom of my management tool bag. And like the doctor's saw, it is the last tool I will use, because once I use the hammer, the rest of the tools are ineffective.

Having to deal with poor employee performance is not a manager's favorite task. Perhaps it is because it is perceived as delivering bad news or as a negative event; perhaps the manager simply does not want to be the bearer of bad news. However, dealing with poor performance should be viewed as an opportunity to increase team effectiveness. The three keys to making it a positive or at least a neutral event lie in how the issue is addressed.

Identify the Performance Issue.

It should be obvious that a manager should never personally criticize an employee nor should he or she attempt to correct performance in front of other team members. The least this will accomplish is to embarrass the employee and create resentment toward you. Stay focused on the specific performance shortfall and avoid blaming. Remember, we want to fix the problem, not assign blame! The first step is to reach agreement on the performance shortfall (not the reasons) with the employee before proceeding.

Identify Reasons for the Shortfall.

Once you reach agreement that there exists a performance shortfall, have the employee identify the reasons for the shortfall and separate the reasons into two categories: (1) those the employee can't control and (2) those the employee can control. If you can assist with those issues beyond the employee's control, offer your assistance. If the issue is also beyond your control, adjust the expected performance to take this into account.

Determine Corrective Actions.

For those issues the employee can control, let the team member determine (within reason) how and when he or she will correct the performance shortfall. If necessary, offer suggestions, being careful not to dictate corrective actions. The worst thing that can happen is for the team members to claim that it was your idea, not theirs, when the corrective action fails. By having the team members take ownership for corrective actions, the odds for successful performance improvement increase significantly. Once the team members have accepted ownership for corrective actions, keep the improvement program in view by establishing periodic follow-up meetings to review progress.

An example of transferring ownership occurred at one point in my career after I had joined a company to manage a division producing high-technology computerized engineering document retrieval systems. The system eliminated the need to deliver paper documents by digitizing the drawings and creating a database of the digitized drawings, thus making the drawings available electronically almost instantaneously at remote locations. The system was software-intensive, and several systems had been delivered to major corporations. Unfortunately, the software was full of bugs and the systems frequently crashed, making them practically unusable.

It turned out that Tom (not his real name), the primary programmer who played a major role in the system's development, had been assigned to install the first system delivered on the customer site and promised a big bonus to get the system up and running. Unfortunately, due to a lack of proper support and despite Tom's best efforts over an extended period of time, the system remained unstable. Tom didn't get the bonus despite his significant effort and felt he had been treated unfairly. Other programmers who were assigned to help debug the system were handicapped because Tom had documented his code in a foreign language and only reluctantly provided support to fellow programmers while spending company time working on forming his own company. Previous management had been reluctant to deal with Tom for fear he would endanger resolving the situation by quitting and therefore treated him with kid gloves.

The original customer was withholding $100,000 final payment and threatening to return the system. I assembled the team, explained how serious the situation had become, and asked them to develop a plan to resolve the problem, which they did. I told them to let me know whatever support they needed and I would do everything I could to get that support. After the meeting, I met with Tom, one-on-one, and asked him if he supported the plan, and he replied that he did. I let him know that I would support him 100 percent and also told him that I knew that he had been dragging his feet in the past while working on his own agenda and that if that behavior continued, he would be terminated. He said he understood, and for the rest of the day, he was actively supporting the team.

But the next morning he came to work and told me he was not interested and was going to quit and form his own company. When I notified the team that Tom had quit, I was surprised when the team said they didn't need Tom to fix the system. I told them I would get whatever they needed, including a translator if necessary. We struck a deal: they would go to the customer site in four weeks and install the new software, and I would negotiate with the customer to give us four weeks' time and pay the $100,000 if we were successful. The customer was livid over the continued promises and delays, but agreed to give us four weeks. To make a long story short, the team installed the software over a weekend, the system came up Monday morning and functioned perfectly, and the customer paid the $100,000.

This is a perfect example of taking corrective action when management was afraid of the consequences of dealing firmly and fairly with the challenge and being held hostage by a passive-aggressive employee. As a manager, you should never allow an employee to hold you or your team hostage. When confronted with this type of situation, ask the question, "What will happen if we do nothing?" Of course, the answer is "If we continue to do what we have always done, we will continue to get what we have always got." This puts the challenge into perspective and provides incentive to eliminate the hostage situation. This may prove scary, but you will find that team members will respect and support you for putting an end to being held hostage. On the flip side, if you don't eliminate the hostage situation, you will lose the team's respect. The choice is yours.

Chapter 15

Poor Performance Decision Tree

Poor performance is readily apparent, but identifying and correcting poor performance can be tricky. Having a checklist or decision tree for identifying and correcting the cause for poor performance makes the task easier and more comprehensive.

Step 0: Is performance adequate?

Yes: No further action required.

No: Go to step (1).

Step 1: Do performance standards exist?

Yes: Go to step (2).

No: Establish performance standards. You can't expect people to perform at or above satisfactory levels if standards have not been established. After performance standards have been established, return to step (0).

Step 2: Have performance standards been communicated?

Yes: Go to step (3).

No: Communicate the performance standards. You may have expectations for satisfactory performance, but have you communicated your expectations to your staff? Most people can't read minds. After standards have been communicated, return to step (0).

Step 3: Are the performance standards understood?

Yes: Go to step (4).

No: Take the time to test for understanding once standards have been communicated. We may understand when we communicate standards for performance, but that does not mean others understand. Test for understanding by observing, asking questions, and so on. Return to step (0).

Step 4: Do people have the skills to perform?

Yes: Go to step (5).

No: Provide training necessary to perform up to standard. Also, keep in mind when hiring to test for necessary skills. Go to step (0).

Step 5: Do people have the necessary resources to perform to standard?

Yes: Go to step (6).

No: Identify missing resources and provide them. If this is not possible, redefine performance expectations to match available resources. Go to step (0).

Step 6: Are corrective action plans in place?

Yes: Go to step (7).

No: Obtain agreement with the employee on the performance shortfall and have the employee submit to you an acceptable goal and corrective action plan to resolve the performance issues. Then track his or her progress on a regular schedule. Let the person define his or her own corrective action plan. Remember, if you dictate the actions, it is your plan, not the employee's. Go to step (0).

Step 7: Do performance consequences exist?

Yes: Implement the consequences.

No: Establish consequences for not correcting performance, as well as for correcting performance. Go to step (0).

Correcting Poor Performance Decision Tree

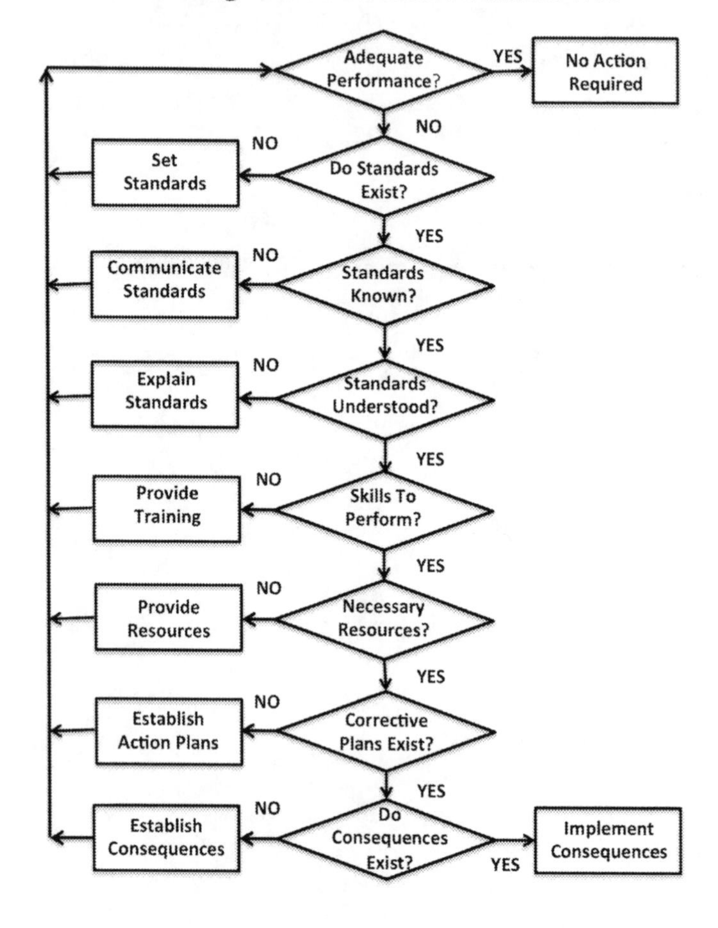

Chapter 16

Preventing the Peter Principle

Preventing the Peter Principle in Yourself.

Preventing the Peter Principle in Your Staff.

Preventing the Peter Principle in Your Organization.

Loosely stated, the Peter Principle states that people rise in the organization until they achieve a position beyond their competence level. You can avoid this principle by following the suggestions below.

Preventing the Peter Principle in Yourself.

This should be the easiest category for preventing future incompetence as you are promoted up the organization. However, it is the one most managers overlook as they concentrate on improving performance in others. The first step in maintaining personal competence as you rise up the corporate ladder is to develop your career plan identifying the positions you are likely to encounter as you progress toward your ultimate career goal. This allows you to identify and acquire ahead of time the knowledge and skill sets necessary to achieve success at each stage. The alternative is struggling to acquire the knowledge and skills simultaneously with having to use them.

Perform a personal assessment of your current knowledge base and skill set on a quarterly basis and identify those areas you need to work on in order to be prepared for the next promotion. In my case, my ultimate career goal was to become president and CEO of an organization, which required me to have a working knowledge of accounting, sales, manufacturing, and engineering. Having advanced through the engineering ranks, I was already knowledgeable in engineering practices but lacking in the other disciplines, so I found ways to acquire knowledge in those other disciplines, through self-study, interacting with personnel in those disciplines, taking formal courses, attending seminars, and so on.

Preventing the Peter Principle in Your Staff.

Equally important as your self-development is developing your team's knowledge and skill sets. Factors similar to those involved in improving your personal competence can help you maintain your staff's competence equal to their tasks. Assess your individual staff member's knowledge and skill set jointly with each staff member, compare it against his or her desired career path, and formally map out a development plan for each staff member to provide knowledge and skill sets necessary for his or her success before they are needed. This serves a triple purpose: (1) it clearly demonstrates that you are interested in your staff members' personal success; (2) by helping them with personal development, you are simultaneously increasing your team's competence level and stimulating increased team productivity, thus enabling you to obtain the reputation as a manager who consistently achieves results; and (3) it builds your team-building skills.

Preventing the Peter Principle in Your Organization.

Just as you and your team members can become incompetent, your organization can also become incompetent and obsolete. Once again, an organizational assessment of future knowledge and skill requirements compared with your organization's current knowledge and skill levels will reveal knowledge and skill deficiencies, such as the need for understanding new technological advancements, developing new manufacturing expertise, different hiring needs, and so on. SWOT charts are useful for this exercise. Set goals to provide your organization with these new needs and begin acquiring them before they are needed.

In summary, preventing the Peter Principle in your organization is as simple as identifying and developing needed future knowledge and skills *ahead of time*. Failure to do this will put you in a position of incompetence, where you are treading water furiously just to keep your head above water, with no time left to develop needed knowledge and skills.

Chapter 17

Correcting Problems: The PGA Process

Identify the Real Problem.

Clearly State the Goal (Solution).

Identify Actions.

It is a rarity for a journey toward a future goal to happen without encountering problems. How effectively managers deal with problems can make a huge difference in results. Oftentimes the manager will attempt to resolve the problem as soon as possible by personally implementing a solution (putting him or her on the path to the danger zone). Perhaps this is the quickest way to resolve a problem, but it may not be the best way and certainly doesn't include the team in the solution. While an individual can generally move faster than a team, the combined brainpower of the team almost always produces a better solution. Here is the three step PGA (Problem–Goal–Action) process for team problem resolution:

Identify the Real Problem.

Before the team is launched into solving the problem, make sure the real problem is identified. Oftentimes, symptoms are identified as the problem, resulting in the symptoms being treated while the fundamental problem remains intact. Getting to the root of a problem is often like peeling an onion, removing layer after layer until the source of the problem is uncovered.

One of my clients was experiencing high manufacturing costs in their product lines. While high manufacturing costs put my client at a competitive disadvantage and was certainly a problem, was it the real problem or a symptom of another problem? Investigation revealed several layers of problems: high failure rates in final circuit-board testing, resulting in excessive technician expense to troubleshoot and repair the boards, wrong components inserted into the boards, and failed solder joints. Thus, the wrong components and poor solder joints created the failures, requiring more technicians and higher costs.

Clearly State the Goal (Solution).

This example clearly illustrates the importance of identifying the real problem before establishing the goal. Once the problem was accurately understood, the goal became obvious: to eliminate wrong component insertion and poor solder joints. Originally the goal had been to repair 100 percent of circuit boards that failed the final test, which resulted in hiring additional technicians and increased manufacturing costs.

Identify Actions.

If a manager identifies the solution to a problem, issues instructions on solving the problem, and doesn't involve his or her staff in helping to solve the problem, he or she effectively guarantees that the problem belongs to him or her. This manager's staff will take less interest in solving the problem and simply do what they are told to do.

In this case, the manufacturing manager wisely involved the manufacturing staff to help identify the actions to realize the goal: to eliminate wrong component insertion and poor solder joints. Several suggestions were put forth, and during the process, it became evident that the staff didn't clearly understand how to identify components for insertion, so if their kits contained the wrong components, the wrong components got inserted into the boards. In addition, the flow solder machine was consistently set up wrong, resulting in the poor solder joints. The staff unanimously agreed that training was required to eliminate these problems. After one week of training and cross-training, the component and soldering problems essentially disappeared.

Had the manager started out by stating that the staff didn't know what they were doing so he was going to train them, he probably would have caused a defensive reaction among his staff and had to force them to follow proper procedures. By involving them in discovering the lack of training, they readily embraced the training and solved the problem.

In another situation, I had an opportunity to witness the wrong way to deal with problems. I had taken our motor home into the dealer to have some repairs made that stretched over two or three days, and we were able to stay in the motor home while the repairs were being made. Evidently the owner had received complaints about repairs getting rescheduled or taking too long, so the service manager assembled his mechanics in one of the service bays near our motor home, well within earshot. I could clearly hear every word that both the service manager and the mechanics were saying.

It was obvious the service manager was angry about getting some flak from the owner about the complaints. The service manager, in an elevated and angry tone, explained to his staff that he was tired of catching flak for the delayed repairs and he wasn't going to put up with any more slacking off, taking too long to finish simple jobs, or time wasted by the crew chewing the fat. It was obvious that he was blaming the crew for the complaints, and he, in no uncertain terms, told the crew that they could either pick up the pace or find another job.

One of the crew attempted to explain that when they were pulled off one job to work on another, the interruption caused the job to take longer. The manager dismissed this as not being part of the problem. He never once asked the crew what they thought could be done to increase job efficiency, or attempted to involve them in solving the problem. He simply stated that the crew was to blame and they needed to shape up or ship out.

We had gotten to know two of the crew fairly well during our stay, and I mentioned to one of them that the service manager seemed to be a little hot under the collar earlier that day. He replied, "Yeah, he gets that way every so often, and we just put up with it. He never listens to us; he just blames us for the problem, so we just let him blow off steam and then go back to work." Further conversation with him revealed that it was common for them to be pulled off one job and reassigned to another depending on the latest crisis. In addition, the training they received consisted of inconsistent word of mouth from mechanic to mechanic as they encountered and solved new problems. There was no formal mechanism for sharing information, such as a weekly meeting for staff to share new things learned during the week.

In this case, the service manager missed a golden opportunity to use the PGA process and unite the crew behind him by sharing the problem and the solutions with the crew. Had he done this, his job would have become a whole lot less lonely and stressful.

Chapter 18

Taking Corrective Action

Identify the Need for Corrective Action.

Determine the Best Corrective Action.

Act Immediately.

Projects rarely go exactly as planned. This is a fact of life, commonly known as Murphy's Law (i.e., If things can go wrong, they will!). How we deal with these deviations from plan can simplify project management or make it a major headache.

Identify the Need for Corrective Action.

Regular project-review meetings quickly and routinely identify deviations from plan and hence the need for corrective action. Set the tone for the review meetings by accepting the fact that deviations are a fact of life and the professional approach is to identify deviations as soon as possible. Remember, the purpose of the meeting is to *fix the problem, not assign blame!*

Determine the Best Corrective Action.

If the corrective action is obvious, do it. If the corrective action is not obvious, use team consulting (brainstorming) to identify possible corrective actions, select the best action, and implement it. (See chapter 17 on the PGA process.)

Act Immediately.

Take immediate corrective action and get back on course ASAP. Do this while the corrective actions required are small and can be accomplished quickly. This seems like it should be obvious, but oftentimes we are distracted and put off taking small corrective actions. Because the required action is small, there is a tendency to put it off until tomorrow. As a result, the deviation from a plan grows larger as time passes. Procrastinating long enough will make the corrective action too large to accomplish in the time frame required to meet project deadlines.

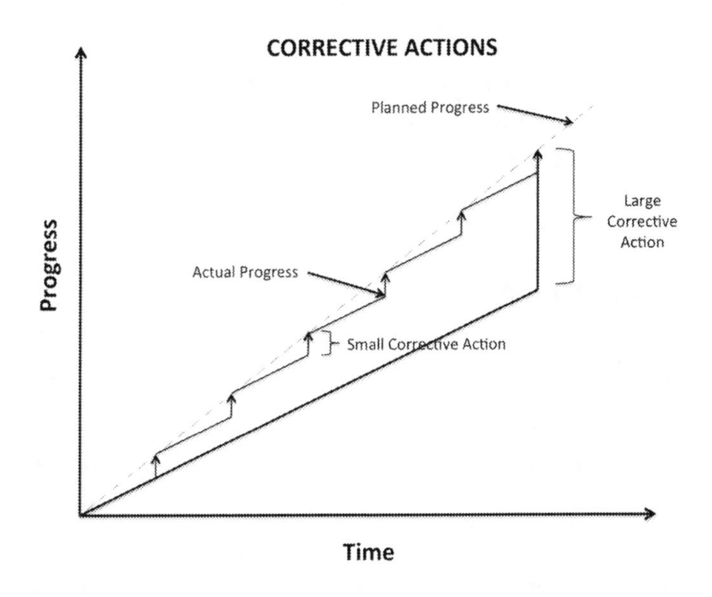

Chapter 19

Establishing Organizational Behavior

Communicate Behavioral Guidelines.

Address Deviations Promptly.

Walk the Talk.

As a manager, you are responsible for your department or organizational behavior. This means how your team behaves relative to others, standards of performance, and ethics. To make sure your organization behaves in the manner you want, three things are necessary.

Communicate Behavioral Guidelines.

Clearly establish in your own mind the behavioral standards you want your organization to exhibit and then clearly communicate these standards. Make sure the standards you set are realistic. Document these standards and make sure all existing and new team members get a copy. A good idea is to create a "behavioral proclamation," which clearly states the organization's desired behaviors. Don't try to document behavior to the nth degree, but rather, provide guidelines that reasonable people can understand.

Address Deviations Promptly.

If deviations from the behavioral standards occur, they must be addressed as soon as they become visible. This makes it clear that the standards are important and deviation will not be tolerated. Not addressing these deviations will make your behavioral standard nothing more than a toothless paper tiger, creating a lack of respect among your staff. This cannot be done selectively. Star performers must be treated the same as all other team members when it comes to following behavioral standards.

Walk the Talk.

One of the most important things a manager can do to ensure adherence to behavioral guidelines is to personally adhere to the guidelines at all times. Nothing destroys credibility faster than team members observing their leader violating the behavioral guidelines. This doesn't mean following the guidelines 98 percent of the time. It means following them 100 percent of the time. If not, then it becomes permissible for team members to observe the guidelines only when it is convenient.

Chapter 20

Reward Results, Not Effort

Clearly Define Expected Results.

Recognize Progress.

Connect Rewards with Results.

The philosophy to reward results, not effort, may sound unfair to team members exerting good effort. However, recognize there is a difference between praising effort and rewarding results. Praising effort is encouragement for trying, while rewarding results is both encouraging and tangible. Rewarding effort sends an implicit message that if employees just try hard, they will be rewarded. When rewards are reserved for those who produce results, people focus on getting results. Continue to recognize team-member effort, because the effort is what eventually gets results. Use the following key tips for rewarding results:

Clearly Define Expected Results.

Clearly defined expectations provide team members with specific targets to shoot for and make it clear when those expectations have been met. Nothing is more discouraging for team members than believing they have met expectations only to be told, "That is not what I meant." If goals (and hence) expected results change, communicate them immediately and give credit for results achieved to date.

Recognize Progress.

Establishing mileposts for goals defines intermediate results, allowing you to recognize and provide interim rewards, allowing for several victories instead of just one. If teams only celebrate when they reach the ultimate goal, celebrations become a rare event.

Connect Rewards with Results.

Do not wait until the next performance review to provide rewards. Whenever possible, give the reward when the result is achieved. Rewards do not have to be monetary. Rewards are a form of recognition, and recognition can take many forms. It can be monetary, extra time off, a pizza party, attending a seminar, a symbolic gift or trophy, and so on.

Chapter 21

Appreciate Your Team

Know Each Team Member.

Encourage Team Members.

Celebrate Team Victories.

As managers, we are constantly facing problems affecting the ability to achieve goals. As Saint Murphy stated, "If something can go wrong, it will." (Anyone who is right as often as Murphy must indeed be a saint!) As a result, it is easy to become "problem-oriented" and focus on problems rather than opportunities. Perhaps the biggest opportunity a manager has is to show appreciation for his or her team and the results they achieve. The following three tips will help you focus on appreciating those who take your career to new heights:

Know Each Team Member.

Appreciating your team begins with knowing each team member. A good coach knows each team member's strengths and weaknesses, as well as what motivates or discourages each team member. Vince Lombardi, coach of the Green Bay Packers, was a master at this, knowing what motivated each of his team members. Armed with this knowledge, he was able to motivate each and every team member. A manager who is able to provide encouragement rather than discouragement and use member strengths to assist in overcoming weaknesses is highly likely to succeed.

Encourage Team Members.

Encouraging team members enhances self-confidence, paving the way for increased performance. When problems arise, it is easy to become *problem-focused* and overlook the opportunity presented by solving the problem. When this happens, the manager often broadcasts discouragement rather than encouragement. It is very easy to identify problems; we all have this special (?) talent, but our duty as managers is to help identify opportunity in the face of adversity. Helping team members to look beyond the problem to spot opportunity automatically provides encouragement.

Celebrate Team Victories.

The most celebrated victory in sports today is arguably the Super Bowl. But that celebration only happens once a year. How drab our world would be with only one celebration per year. The message here is to celebrate the victories (achieved milestones) as they occur, rather than waiting for project completion. This not only creates more fun in the work environment, but it also provides motivation for team members to produce results. The celebration doesn't necessarily have to rival Super Bowl parties, but the celebration needs to occur. It may be as simple as a hosted pizza party at the local pizza parlor or as nice as a formal dinner party hosting team members and their spouses or significant others.

I once provided one dozen long-stemmed roses to team members' spouses and significant others after dessert at a team dinner. Five years later, a team member told me his wife still remembered that event. Another technique I have used is to have my software development team train the sales force on new product releases, followed by a dinner cruise on San Diego Bay for the programmers, their spouses and significant others, and the sales force. The programmers loved being able to strut their stuff while training the sales staff and to get positive feedback about all the cool new features in the new release. It also provided a venue to invite other support personnel to the dinner cruise, thus putting faces with names and building team spirit among the team members.

Always remember: the ship that takes you on your career journey is your team. You will get there faster if they feel like pulling on the oars.

Chapter 22

Ask for Success

Review Goal Successes.

Bank on People's Desire to Win.

Provide an Environment for Success.

As managers, we are required to achieve results, on time and within budget. We do this through team efforts, not our own personal effort. We use such tools as setting goals for team members as well as the team, having regular project-review meetings, checking progress toward goals, holding people accountable, encouraging results, and so on. While we need results to meet goals, consider asking for success as well as results. This may sound redundant, but letting people tout their success can be a powerful motivational tool. Consider three reasons to ask for success:

Review Goal Successes.

An alternative to asking team members to report the results for the time period between project-review meetings is to ask the team members to report their successes for the time period. This will put a positive spin on the project-review meeting as people tout their success rather than listening to shortfalls, missed deadlines, and so on. By doing this, people are motivated to share their success and will be reluctant to come to the meeting without at least some success to report.

Bank on People's Desire to Win.

Have you ever met a person who wants to lose? Neither have I. So let's build this desire into the way we review progress toward goals. People will work harder to be able to share their success than they will to avoid embarrassment for failure. In addition, it will become a team mentality to focus on success (rather than excuses). Once this focus on success becomes a team mentality, an amazing thing happens: morale soars. Winning organizations have good morale; losing organizations have poor morale.

Provide an Environment for Success.

Talk to others about the team member's successes and to the organization about the team's successes. Become a manager who focuses on success and encourages innovative ways to overcome obstacles to achieve that success. Encourage staff members who are having difficulty; make sure they have the tools to succeed, including materials and resources. Work to support your team's success and to provide an environment in which success is probable rather than accidental. Overcommitting team members will guarantee failure, so make sure individual team goals are attainable.

Chapter 23

Focus on Strengths

Recognize Team Member Strengths.

Don't Be Judgmental.

Be Complimentary.

As a manager, you are responsible for dealing with problems and correcting them. Since projects rarely go according to plan, continually taking corrective action is the norm. However, this creates the tendency for managers to focus on what's wrong rather than what's right. This tendency in many cases unfortunately carries over to how a manager views his team. Obviously the manager has to deal with team deficiencies, sometimes creating more of a focus on team member weaknesses rather than team member strengths. This can create a perception among team members that the manager does not appreciate them. To avoid this, try the following three actions:

Recognize Team Member Strengths.

Let each of your team members know that you are aware of and appreciate their strong points. Support them in their efforts to improve themselves by offering training and coaching, giving them opportunity to grow with assignments that foster growth, and so on. When conducting performance reviews, start on a positive note by itemizing what you appreciate about them before suggesting areas for improvement.

Don't Be Judgmental.

When dealing with performance shortfalls, make sure you also recognize what the person is doing right. Remember: good managers fix problems, not assign blame. Don't be judgmental. Stick to the disparity between actual and expected results. Listen to the explanation for the shortfall and offer to help in those areas where your assistance is necessary. Let people tell you how they plan to improve performance (rather than telling them what to do) and be supportive. In other words, let them own their improved performance plan by making it their victory rather than yours.

Be Complimentary.

Do not wait to provide compliments for good results. Be spontaneous. Whenever you see positive results, let the person know that you know how well he or she is doing. Project confidence in people's abilities. Don't become known as a manager who only recognizes mistakes.

Chapter 24

Focus on Encouragement

Eliminate Discouragement.

Improve Morale.

Foster Success.

The effective manager stays focused on his or her top three priorities at all times. One of the priorities that might qualify as one of the top three is encouragement. People who are encouraged usually accomplish exceptional results. The opposite is also true, that is, discouraged people seldom produce exceptional results. Stated this way, it becomes obvious that managers should not let encouragement be a random event. There are three key reasons for focusing on encouragement:

Eliminate Discouragement.

When you set the example of encouraging others, discouragement gradually disappears. Discouragement is like a virus infecting a team and affects the results it produces. Once it takes hold, it is very difficult to eliminate, so make sure you don't let it take root in your organization by becoming discouraged yourself. You may feel discouraged, but showing it only spreads it, never eliminates it. There is always a positive opportunity, even if it is not immediately obvious. Make the effort to help the team find it.

Improve Morale.

By encouraging team members, you're maximizing the team's chances of winning. Teams that are winning invariably have high levels of morale, while losing teams suffer from poor morale. High team morale results in team members encouraging and supporting each other, rather than griping and blaming each other. Morale increases when people are encouraged to try new techniques, even if it involves some level of risk. They feel trusted to not let the team down and will go the extra mile to ensure results, as well as feeling empowered to try their very best.

Foster Success.

Recruiters look for candidates who explain how they achieve success rather than offering excuses for failure. An encouraging atmosphere allows people to take chances, to go the extra step without fear of recrimination. This, in turn, produces better results, resulting in more self-confidence and higher levels of pride. Ask team members to share their successes at team meetings in addition to broadcasting their successes outside your own team. Low morale spawns a downward spiral; high levels of morale spawn upward spirals. Which do you want for your team? Remember: you set the example by being an encouraging person.

Chapter 25

Keys for Effective Leadership

Communicate Clearly Defined Missions and Objectives.

Encourage and Support Followers.

Exhibit Confidence.

Leaders have willing followers. *Why?*

How do you know if you are an effective leader? Simple: look behind you and see if you have willing followers. The key word is *willing*. People may be following you out of necessity, that is, they report to you, they need the paycheck, they fear the consequences of not following, and so on. True leaders have followers who want to follow! So how do leaders get willing followers? The following three factors are critical:

Communicate Clearly Defined Missions and Objectives.

Followers need to feel a sense of purpose and accomplishment if they are to continue following a leader. Without clearly defined missions and objectives, it is impossible to measure progress, and therefore winning and losing become fuzzy. The true leader defines and clearly communicates ethical missions and objectives. These may be extremely difficult, but personnel will follow if they understand the mission's or objective's necessity. A charismatic person may be fun to follow, but without progress, people lose their sense of accomplishment and their interest in following.

Encourage and Support Followers.

Leaders listen! George Washington encouraged and listened to his staff's input, not necessarily to follow their input, but by knowing all the input, he knew more than others about given situations. Key words here are *encourage* and *support*. This means the encouragement and support are genuinely given to those who produce results.

Followers want to win, and they do not want to associate with and be dragged down by nonperformers! (When was the last time you saw an eagle in a flock of turkeys?) For those who don't produce results, feedback needs to be direct, fair, honest, and encouraging. Allowing continued failure to perform by a team member will undermine all efforts to encourage the remaining team members. Continued failure to perform should lead to dismissal from the team.

Exhibit Confidence.

Leaders act like leaders. Who wants to follow a person who lacks confidence? Leaders know the importance of exhibiting confidence, even when they don't feel confident. They know that confidence is contagious. They know that others quickly pick up on a leader's lack of confidence. Along these same lines, leaders show no fear even when afraid, they show no hunger even when hungry, they never complain even when they feel like complaining, and so on. *Fake it until you make it* might be appropriate in these situations. Leaders recognize they are role models for followers and consistently behave in a manner they expect from their followers.

Being confident includes demonstrating confidence in your staff's abilities. When you express that confidence, staff members will be reluctant to not meet your expressed confidence. Recognize the fact that people want to succeed. If they don't, try to understand why and try to correct it. (Perhaps they never bought into the goals that have been set or they lack self-confidence.)

Chapter 26

People Rules for Managers

Be Careful How You Talk about People.

Look for *Ways* to Help Other People.

Don't Give Unsolicited *Advice*.

It seems as if we have more than enough rules to follow in today's management environment, and these rules regarding what we can do and what we can't do are usually spelled out very clearly. In human resources, there are people rules, such as how often to give performance reviews, disciplinary rules, salary levels, and so on. But what are the unwritten people rules for managers? Here are three good common-sense rules:

Be Careful How You Talk about People.

Never talk negatively about a person to other personnel, no matter how you personally feel about the individual. This is a sure way to lose respect. The old saying "If you can't say something good about a person, don't say anything at all" is a golden rule. Face it: people talk to other people, and what you say to one person about another person often finds its way back to the other person. Even if it doesn't get back to that person, the person you talk to will wonder, *If you talk about others this way, what are you saying about me?* If an issue with an individual needs correcting, discuss it with that individual on a one-on-one basis.

Look for Ways to Help Other People.

Helping others is a surefire way to enhance your reputation. You don't have to wait to be asked; rather, ask if you can help. People have a tendency to repay favors, and you never know when you might need a favor. In addition, people will talk to others about you as a manager. What would you like them to say about you? I would prefer that people describe me as a person who is always willing to go out of my way to help others.

Don't Give Unsolicited Advice.

Unless it is in regard to a direct report's performance, don't give unsolicited feedback or advice to others. For direct reports, you are expected to do this, but make sure you do it in a supportive manner if at all possible. Giving unsolicited advice to people who do not report directly to you is often interpreted as criticism, labeling you as a negative critic (i.e., Who asked him or her?). If people ask for your advice, feel free to give it, but if their opinion differs from yours, don't try to convince them that your advice is the right way or only way.

Chapter 27

Team Motivation Factors

Involve the Team in Setting the Goals.

Identify Responsibilities.

Identify *What's in It for Them?* (*WIIFT*).

We all know that setting goals is vital to our success as managers. However, how these goals are set is vital to achieving them. If the team isn't fully committed to achieving the goals, the chance for success is greatly diminished. So how do we get the team fully committed? The following three key factors go a long way toward getting that commitment:

Involve the Team in Setting the Goals.

The worst thing that can happen to you as a manager is for the team to perceive that the goals are yours, not theirs. This doesn't mean abdicating your responsibility as a manager by not establishing goals, but rather setting an initial goal and then involving the team in a brainstorming session. In this session, you want the team to discuss whether the goal is realistic (consider goal magnitude and time frame), the different ways to achieve the goal (strategy), and specific tasks necessary to achieve the goal (tactics). Listen to the team during this process and be willing to accept better ideas than your own. The goal for this session is to emerge with a set of good goals (characterized by quantity, quality, cost, and time) that the team understands and can commit to.

If upper management has dictated your team's goals, explain to the team that is what you've been asked to achieve and use the brainstorming session to determine strategy and tactics to maximize the probability of success. If upper management has set unrealistic goals, don't try to convince the team that the goals are realistic or you will lose credibility. Simply say, "Let's figure out how to give it our best shot." With this attitude, the team may just surprise themselves on how much they can accomplish.

Identify Responsibilities.

Give the members a chance to volunteer before assigning responsibilities. People who *want* to do something are more motivated than people who *have* to do something. Once responsibilities have been assigned, make sure individual responsibilities are visible to the entire team to eliminate duplication of effort and maximize support by and for individual team members. An added benefit to creating this visibility is team members who know they are visible want to make sure they succeed with their responsibilities and not be the one to let the team down.

Once responsibilities are identified, let team members determine how they will achieve their individual responsibilities. Even though you have ideas on how things should be done, let people determine how they will do it. You can ask how they plan to accomplish their tasks, but unless you are convinced it won't work, let them do it their way. You might express your concern about their method, but the bottom line is that they will work ten times harder to prove their way will work than to implement your suggestions.

Identify What's in It for Them? (WIIFT).

People are motivated to perform their jobs for a variety of basic reasons (Maslow's hierarchy of needs, for example: physiological, safety, love and belonging, self-esteem, self-actualization). Employed personnel have generally met most of their safety and physiological (food, water, shelter, etc.) needs. So these needs, having been satisfied, provide little additional motivation. However, the job doesn't always provide for the next three levels of need: belonging, self-esteem, and self-actualization. Managers who encourage and foster teamwork go a long way toward satisfying the need to belong in the work environment. Team members appreciate support from the team and return that support to the team. The reverse is equally true.

The next need level is self-esteem, that is, self-respect. Being respected by others goes a long way to developing and maintaining self-respect, and self-respect leads to self-confidence. As a manager, respect your team members for their strengths, rather than lacking respect for them because of their shortcomings.

Finally team members want self-actualization, that is, doing what they are really good at. Once again, to the extent possible, let team members determine how they will accomplish tasks rather than telling them. Look for and allow team members to use their special talents. There are lots of ways to compliment the WIIFT factors through support for individual team members. A team member undergoing a family crisis may need some time off or flexibility in working hours. A bonus for a job well done can be in the form of extra pay, time off, attendance at a seminar, and so on. Recognizing a spouse for supporting your team member's extra time commitment to get the job done on time can reduce tension on the home front. Make the effort to be in tune with each team member's special situation, and recognition kudos will become apparent.

In summary, ask yourself if you are involving your team in the goal-setting process (i.e., planning), if you are allowing team members to determine how they will accomplish their tasks, and finally, if you are addressing the WIIFT factor.

Chapter 28

Motivating Team Members

Don't Micromanage.

Give the Team All the Credit.

Be Sincere.

As a manager, you are responsible for results, not only your own results but also the results of others. It is the team results as well as your own results that will determine how successful you will be. Communicating your appreciation for your team goes a long way to ensure above-average results. When your team feels appreciated, they are more motivated to excel. On the flip side, if they feel unappreciated, you can expect mediocre performance, just enough to keep their job until they can find something better. To make sure your team feels appreciated, follow the following three guidelines:

Don't Micromanage.

Constantly looking over your team's shoulders and directing all aspects of the tasks will tell your team that you don't trust them. Clearly communicate expectations for final results, and let the team use their ideas to achieve these results. At most, you might ask the team how they plan to accomplish the final results. Even though it may be different from how you might do it, if you can see that it can work, let go and let the team show you how well it can be done.

Give the Team All the Credit.

Never take credit for others' accomplishments. Make sure you acknowledge the team's results not only to the team but also to the rest of the organization. Recognize individual contributions as well as the team's results. Make sure your team knows that you are their best fan. Celebrate your team's victories as they occur. Don't wait until the entire project is completed. Keep the celebrations fun and varied.

Be Sincere.

Be sincere in giving the team credit for results. When praising or rewarding, make sure it is deserved and not just shallow words. Encourage effort, but praise and reward results. Let individual team members know that you appreciate their contributions and take a personal interest in them. Do not give credit when credit is not due, or you will make words of credit hollow.

Chapter 29

Why People Quit

Poor Relationship with One's Immediate Manager.

Lack of Support.

Inadequate Compensation.

One of the most disruptive events a manager faces is when a key employee quits. Once that employee announces his or her decision to leave, it is almost impossible to reverse that decision. When was the last time an employee told you he or she was thinking of quitting? Probably never! This reflects a person's basic instinct: self-preservation. Once an employee quits, a hole is left in your organization, and you will have to devote effort to replace that employee and remove the hole. This is effort that could have been directed toward your vital few. So why do people quit? Listed here are three primary reasons people quit:

Poor Relationship with One's Immediate Manager.

A poor relationship with one's immediate manager will almost always foster thoughts of quitting and seeking employment elsewhere, either in a different company or in another organization within the same company. A poor relationship can be the result of a myriad of different reasons—for example, feeling unappreciated, being micromanaged, being treated with a lack of respect, and so on.

These reasons are often overlooked by the supervising manager, and thus, he or she is caught by surprise when the employee resigns. A primary reason for this lack of recognition is not taking the time to communicate with the employee and getting to know how that employee feels about things.

Lack of Support.

This can include a lack of support from one's manager or the organization, lack of necessary or adequate tools to perform required tasks, and failure to recognize and support an individual's personal and professional goals. Making sure the employee is recognized for the results he or she achieves might be merely a pat on the back or an unexpected bonus. In the public sector, where a bonus may not be feasible, selecting the employee to attend a seminar or represent the organization at an important meeting can be a way to provide recognition. Regarding lack of support from the organization, working with the employees and representing their valid support needs to upper management at least lets the employees know you are on their side.

Nothing is more frustrating than being asked to do a job without adequate tools—especially when it is common knowledge that adequate tools exist but aren't being provided. This can range from needed support staff to ineffective or outdated software.

In addition to giving recognition for achieving results and providing necessary tools, go the extra mile and support team members' personal and professional goals. Take the time to learn about their personal and professional aspirations and look for ways to support them. This demonstrates interest on a personal level as well as a professional level.

Inadequate Compensation.

Failure to compensate employees in a fair and competitive manner will eventually lead to their checking out other positions with a more lucrative compensation package. In today's environment of abundant information, people know what their job is worth and what benefits are being provided by other organizations. While enjoying one's work, the work environment, and associates is important for retaining employees, lack of fair and adequate compensation undermines these factors. Stay in tune with what competitive compensation packages exist. If the wage scale is set by your organization, be proactive to make sure your wage scales are, at a minimum, competitive.

Chapter 30

Retaining Key Employees

Take a Personal Interest.

Support Them.

Let Them Do Their Job.

Finding and developing key employees is not a simple matter, and once you have key employees, make the effort to retain them. Perhaps the most significant factor for retaining key employees is the relationship between the employee and his or her manager. A poor employee-manager relationship almost certainly leads to employees seeking ways to depart. On the other hand, a good, strong manager-employee relationship provides added incentive for key employee loyalty. The following three factors go a long way to developing that strong relationship:

Take a Personal Interest.

First and foremost, employees are more than just warm bodies. They are people with human needs and wants. This includes the need for recognition, respect, fair and equitable treatment, understanding of personal matters, career ambitions, and so on.

Taking a personal interest is something you make happen. It is easy to overlook this factor in today's demanding environment, and unless you schedule time to work on these relationships, they probably won't develop. Take the time to assist employees with their career goals; learn about their families, their spouse's first name, their children and their names and birthdays, and so on. Be sensitive to personal factors affecting them, such as new family arrivals, personal crisis such as a death or injury in the family, and so on. By doing these things, employees know you care about them as people in addition to their contribution as employees.

Support Them.

Make sure your employees have the tools to do the job they are being asked to do. Nothing is more frustrating than attempting to accomplish anything without the proper tools or resources. This not only means the proper hardware and software but also realistic time frames to get the job done. Provide encouragement not only when they are succeeding but also when they encounter difficulty. Be available if they need to talk or seek advice. Be sensitive to, and support them on, factors in their personal life, like an illness in the family, new additions, financial crises, and so on. These efforts will be rewarded with loyalty.

Let Them Do Their Job.

Finally, let them do their job. Get out of the way. Trust them to accomplish goals they have committed to. Don't micromanage them by checking up on them continually. Rather, establish agreed-upon intervals to review progress and let them tell you how they are doing. Once again, recognize their accomplishments and support their needs. Never take credit for their accomplishments.

Remember: your employees determine your success or failure just as much or even more than your own efforts.

These principles were the key ingredients discovered during one of my consulting assignments with a large multinational company to uncover reasons for higher-than-normal management turnover. I interviewed current management personnel nationwide, as well as managers who had recently resigned. Nearly all cited at least one of these key factors about one senior vice president. These factors were also present when I interviewed nonmanagement personnel. I presented my findings to the VP over breakfast, and he was totally taken aback. He had no inkling of how he was perceived in the organization and thought he was doing a great job, even though he was one of the major reasons for the turnover. To his credit, he accepted the feedback and changed his behavior.

This story was repeated time and time again during workshops conducted by my company. The workshops included an anonymous (contributors were not identified) 360 review for all participants, whereby each participant was given a verbatim copy of comments coworkers had made. We found that the anonymity factor allowed contributors to truthfully and candidly speak their minds.

Participants truly interested in self-improvement didn't try to rationalize the feedback, accepted it for what it was, and developed self-improvement action plans. In some cases, participants were aware of their need for improvement but didn't think it was visible to others (*wrong!*). Some chose to rationalize the feedback by dismissing it as coming from people who were misinformed or just plain wrong. Misinformed or wrong, the feedback given was the reality for the persons giving the feedback, and it was up to the participants to correct that perception, either through better communications or by changing their behavior.

The only feedback in the 360 review that identified the contributor was from the participant's direct manager (who knew in advance his feedback would be shared). Oftentimes participants were totally unaware of their manager's perception relative to their performance. For some reason, some managers didn't share their thoughts with their employees.

With these examples of disconnect between a person's self-appraisal and the appraisal of others (including his or her manager) is it any wonder people struggle to succeed? This makes knowing how you are perceived in your organization one of the vital few factors for your success.

Remember: you may be the last to know why your career is on hold if you are not open to or do not seek feedback.

Chapter 31

Building and Maintaining Trust

What Builds Trust.

What Destroys Trust.

Relation between Values and Trust.

What is trust? According to the *American Heritage Dictionary of the English Language*, *trust* is "The condition and resulting obligation of having confidence placed in one. To rely, depend, have confidence in. To expect with assurance." Put simply, trust in others is literally being confident they will perform in an expected manner. However, the most accepted definition of trust is being confident that others will perform/behave in an expected and acceptable manner (where *acceptable* means acceptable to me). The following three items relate to trust in common management environments:

What Builds Trust.

Trust is based on honesty, integrity, behavior in accordance with one's expectations, and dependability. This means delivering what has been promised, delivering when it is promised, and consistently delivering quality. Trust is built up over time, and the more consistently these items are experienced, the stronger the trust becomes. When trust is strong enough, a handshake will seal a deal. If it is not strong enough, a contract is usually required. Consistency is critical in building trust with others, especially your staff.

What Destroys Trust.

Trust is destroyed when one exhibits inconsistent behavior, overcommits, lies, steals, cheats, and so on. In the realm of trust, the adage "One aw shit destroys 1,000 attaboys" is especially true. Even though it diminishes with ongoing consistent behavior, one inconsistency will always cast some shadow of doubt.

Relation between Values and Trust.

Behavior in accordance with shared values is the foundation for complete trust. Without shared values, building trust becomes difficult, if not impossible. With partially shared values, partial trust (in the acceptable sense) is possible where the values overlap. In the literal sense, you can trust someone to perform in a certain way inconsistent with your values. However, without shared values, you probably would not want that person on your team.

As a manager, trust among your team members is essential, which implies an obligation on your part to work with your team to define and adhere to common team values. Don't leave this critical item to chance. To build trust, it is critical for a manager to *walk the talk* at all times!

Chapter 32

Your Respect Rating

Always Tell the Truth.

Put Others' Needs Ahead of Your Own.

Define Your Ethical Standards and Walk the Talk.

To be an effective manager, you need to have the respect of all your team members. As a rule, the feedback you receive during a performance review with your manager usually only includes performance ratings, not how well you are respected. In general, your respect rating, although real, usually remains invisible to you. The grapevine, however, carries your respect rating to all team members. This respect significantly affects the amount of support you will get from others and can be quantified by (1) obtaining an independent and anonymous 360 review by your teammates and (2) rating yourself candidly and honestly in the following three key factors:

Always Tell the Truth.

If you object to something, don't be afraid to say, "I disagree." Otherwise, people might think you agree, only to be disappointed later on when they find out you don't agree. People need to clearly know where you stand and what you think.

When evaluating your staff's performance, be honest. Do this in a tactful way by staying focused on performance results, rather than personal factors. Telling the truth doesn't mean being blunt; take into account others' feelings and be tactful.

Put Others' Needs Ahead of Your Own.

You will succeed or fail depending on the support you get from your team members. Managers who always put their needs ahead of others' are sure to lose respect. With that loss of respect comes a loss of support, and in the worst case, sabotage. By demonstrating consistent concern and support for team members, you will earn respect. (*Note: you cannot demand respect; you can only earn it.*)

Define Your Ethical Standards and Walk the Talk.

People are quick to pick up on others' behavior. What's more, they talk about their observations to others who haven't observed, spreading perceptions about you. This can either undermine your respect or enhance it. It is critical for a manager to have a solid foundation of ethical behavior. Take the time to define what your ethical standards will be, and then make sure you live up to your standards (i.e., walk the talk).

In each of the following three criteria, rate yourself on the percentage of time you meet the criteria:

> What percentage of time do you tell the truth?
>
> What percentage of time do you put others' needs ahead of your own?
>
> What percentage of time do you walk the talk?

This self-rating will give you a means to quantify your respect rating between 0 percent and 100 percent and compare it to an independent and anonymous 360-feedback review.

Chapter 33

Critical Managerial Behaviors

Always Be Sincere.

Walk the Talk.

Don't Spread Rumors.

As a manager, you are always on stage, not only in front of your direct reports but also your management, your peers, and others in your organization. How you behave is critical to your success. Here are three behaviors every manager should exhibit:

Always Be Sincere.

Say what you mean and mean what you say (in a tactful manner, of course). Give credit when credit is due, and never flatter someone insincerely to gain favor. This shallow behavior is very transparent and will make you look like an insincere brownnoser. If you are not sure, admit that you are not sure. By adamantly being sincere at all times, you will gain people's trust in what you say and do. Trust is the behavioral prerequisite to being a successful manager.

When I was an engineering manager whose group was in competition to win a prototype contract, the client asked me, "What is the probability that your prototype will meet specifications by the deadline?" I answered, "Ninety-five percent." The next question was, "What is the probability that your first production units will meet specifications by the deadline?" to which I replied, "Eighty-five percent." Several people in that meeting were shocked by my answer, believing the customer wanted to hear the opposite odds. I explained my rationale as follows: "We can control and tweak one unit more easily than we can control and tweak an entire production line in a given time frame."

While many people were uncomfortable with my 85 percent answer, it was later found out that the competition had answered the questions with the reverse percentages: 85 percent to get the prototype to perform to specifications on time, and 95 percent to get the production run to meet specifications on time. The client agreed with my assessment and awarded my team the contract. By telling the truth, we gained the client's trust and won the contract.

Walk the Talk.

This phrase is certainly overused, but that doesn't make it any less true. This is not always easy, but it is absolutely necessary to earn the respect of others. Nothing will destroy trust faster than people hearing you say one thing and then seeing you doing something else. In the above example, I was known for telling the truth, while the competitor felt it was more important to downplay the risks of getting a production run to meet specifications than to tell the obvious truth.

If you don't know something, don't try to bluff your way through, acting as if you do know. There is usually someone in the crowd who knows the answer and knows that you don't know! In this case, the customer knew and awarded the contract to the manager who told the truth.

Don't Spread Rumors.

In your career, you will hear many rumors. Let the rumor stop with you. Don't pass it on. Verify the facts to ensure that you are not spreading rumors. Once again, if you don't know, say you don't know. On the other hand, be prepared to substantiate what you believe to be the truth. Following this simple rule will ensure that people will believe what you say, rather than wondering if what you say is fact or rumor.

The Internet is a great example of how rumor easily poses as truth, and how willing people are to believe these rumors, consistently forwarding the rumors to their entire mailing list. I have heard it said that 85 percent of the Internet content is rumor. While I cannot substantiate this figure, I wouldn't be the least bit surprised if it were true.

Chapter 34

Getting Organized

Organize Your Time.

Organize Your Work.

Organize Your Career.

Good organization greatly improves the ability to get things done properly and on time. It all starts with getting yourself organized. If you're not organized, for sure your organization will not be well organized. For any manager with a future, there are three key factors for getting organized:

Organize Your Time.

With clearly defined goals, it is easy to determine if your time is well organized. Simply ask yourself, "Is this activity vital to achieving my goals?" If not, why are you doing it? Does it leave enough time to achieve your goals? The first step is to analyze how you are spending your time. Second, plan your time to utilize it in the most effective manner to achieve your goals. Third, eliminate time wasters from your activities.

Organize Your Work.

There are certain items your management expects you to perform or complete. Make sure you are organized to meet these expectations first. Not doing this will definitely earn you demerits. Next, allow time to perform those tasks that you must perform, such as making sure goals and plans for your department are in place, establishing a system to monitor progress, and devoting time to support your staff. Finally, allow time to develop your staff through regular performance reviews, training, and coaching.

Organize Your Career.

Have a career goal, a career plan, and a determination to maintain work-life balance. Know what your ultimate career goal is and the intermediate steps to get there. Plan to acquire the skills needed to achieve the intermediate steps (positions). Determine your vital personal life factors that you will not allow work to interfere with. Some suggestions are your health, quality family time, vacations, and so on.

Chapter 35

Lateral Thinking

Looking Sideways.

Consequential Thinking.

Implementation Alternatives.

Normal thinking is usually straight ahead, task-oriented, and "me"-oriented. It is very much focused on the task at hand, the immediate requirements to get the job done, and personal impact. Lateral thinking does not exclude these factors, but goes beyond by looking sideways, considering the consequences of actions, and exploring different ways and methods by thinking outside the box.

Looking Sideways.

Keep an eye on what is happening around you in addition to what is happening in front of you. Your project may be progressing as planned, but lateral factors (such as the economy, new technology, etc.) may be omens of danger.

Consequential Thinking.

Consequential thinking considers the impact that actions will have (on the environment, other organizations, people, etc.). In other words, it takes into account the impact plans and actions will have outside the immediate realm of the current project.

It considers whether or not the impacts will be beneficial or harmful. Consequential thinking in past decades could have minimized some of the environmental concerns the world is facing today.

Implementation Alternatives.

Lateral thinking explores alternative ways of getting it done. It takes into account three important aspects:

> *Vertical Resources*: Resources I control, as well as those my manager controls.
>
> *Horizontal Resources*: These may include resources controlled by the company, who my manager knows, who my company knows, acquaintances, friends, relatives, vendors, customers, and so on.
>
> *Examination of Other Ways*: How other companies have done it, how other people have done it, getting outside the envelope, and so on.

A famous example of lateral thinking outside the box was exhibited by Robert Ballard, who discovered the *Titanic* in less than twelve days of searching after others had spent years searching for the famous wreck. He abandoned the traditional underwater search technique of using narrow search sweeps to find the main wreck. Instead, he searched for the debris trail left by the sinking ship using much wider sweeps, which allowed him to cover a much larger area in a much shorter time frame. Once he discovered the debris trail, it was a simple matter to follow it to the wreck.

Chapter 36

Eliminating Personal Weakness

Identify Your Weaknesses.

Prioritize According to Your Goals.

Take Corrective Action.

We all have strengths and weaknesses. While we are usually aware of our strengths, the same may not be true of our weaknesses. Eliminating our weaknesses is just as important as enhancing our strengths. Consider these three key steps for eliminating weaknesses:

Identify Your Weaknesses.

Oftentimes we have blind spots and are the last to know some of our weaknesses. People are reluctant to point out our weaknesses, so we need to be proactive in seeking others' observations and opinions.

A 360 review is an excellent mechanism to get this feedback. This is usually accomplished with the aid of a neutral third party (a personal or management consultant, for example), who can compile feedback while offering anonymity to people providing feedback. The anonymity factor helps ensure candor in the feedback. Accept the feedback realistically. Don't dismiss it or rationalize it away.

One of my clients tried to dismiss others' opinions in his 360 review as coming from people who didn't matter to him. When asked if he thought that these people might be sharing their opinions with other people in the organization, including his manager, he came to the stark realization that unflattering comments about him were being spread without his knowledge. Since then, he takes the feedback much more seriously.

Prioritize According to Your Goals.

After identifying weaknesses, prioritize them in accordance with your goals. Which are having the greatest and the least impact on your ability to achieve your goals? Take the top three weaknesses and devise a plan to eliminate or neutralize them. Limit yourself to no more than three to keep your efforts realistic and achievable. Find a confidant and ask him or her to give you candid feedback on your progress. Assess your progress on a weekly basis. At the end of the week, make yourself a list of what you accomplished, didn't accomplish, or lost ground with, and set your goals for the following week.

Take Corrective Action.

Overcoming bad habits is not easily accomplished, so don't get discouraged if you occasionally regress. Set yourself realistic time frames to accomplish improvement. Making yourself accountable to a third party is excellent motivation for overcoming weaknesses. Let your confidant in on your plans and meet with him on a regular basis to get his feedback on your progress. For example, to hold myself accountable when I quit smoking, I told all my associates that I had quit, knowing how embarrassed I would be if I failed.

Chapter 37

Becoming Indispensable

Be a Top Performer.

Be Dependable.

Support Goals.

Unless you are fortunate enough to be independently wealthy, a regular paycheck is vital to your lifestyle, not to mention survival. When the economy is robust, job security is not usually a concern. But when the economy takes a downturn, unemployment goes up. So how do you maximize the probability of staying employed? By being indispensable. Here are three key tips for becoming indispensable:

Be a Top Performer.

Top performers know how well they are performing and what they need to improve. They continually strive to improve all aspects of their performance. They know their weak points and work hard to overcome their weaknesses. When it's time to trim staff, managers try to keep the top performers and eliminate marginal performers. If you are a top performer, strive to become even better.

If you're not a top performer, focus on your performance. Don't make excuses for your weaknesses. Accept them as fact, and work at overcoming them through training and practice. Seek out a mentor or confidant who will provide you with honest assessments. Listen to the feedback others may give you, both verbal and nonverbal.

Be Dependable.

Make sure your manager and others know that they can depend on you to meet your assignments and goals on time and within budget. Be there when you are needed. Go the extra mile, rather than just doing enough to get by. Ask, "What can I do to help?" rather than thinking, "That's not my job." Volunteer rather than waiting to be asked or assigned to do a task. Staying focused on the vital few is absolutely necessary to doing this.

Support Goals.

Actively support not only your manager's goals but also departmental and corporate goals. Make sure your goals are aligned with the goals of upper-level management and are met on time. Don't limit your support to simply achieving your goals, but offer assistance to others in meeting their goals.

Complying with these three tips consistently will establish a good track record. Once downsizing is a reality, it is too late to change your track record. Make sure your work exceeds expectations, be reliable, be willing to lend a helping hand, and understand and support management goals (this includes keeping a positive attitude). Remember: you can't control the economy, but you can control your performance and attitude.

Chapter 38

Communications Advice

Written Communications Advice.

Verbal Communications Advice.

Visual Communications Advice.

We can all agree that communicating is vital for effective management. There are three types of communication, two of which are obvious and one that is not so obvious but just as real. The obvious are written and verbal communication. The not so obvious is the visual communication we all exhibit in one form or another. Below I provide three tips about these forms of communication.

Realize that different people relate differently to these three forms of communication. Some people are "reader-writers" and prefer written communication. Others are more effective with verbal input and often ignore written communications. And finally, some people prefer visualizing the communications. Determine which class of recipient you are dealing with in order to choose the most effective communication style.

Written Communications Advice.

Written communication gives you the chance to edit your communication before you send it. Thus, it should be the most accurate form of communication, clearly conveying intended meanings. However, this is not always the case. To achieve this, it helps to develop your vocabulary, use simple sentences that are easily understood, not be overly verbose, and recap the message at the end. Even so, people will interpret the same communiqué in different ways. It is a good idea to have one or two others read the communiqué and give you feedback prior to sending.

Verbal Communications Advice.

With verbal communication, once it is said, it can't be edited, reedited, or canceled. And it can't be taken back, even if you state you didn't mean it or you apologize for saying it. The fact that it was said still exists. And the recipient can't put the communiqué in his or her in-basket to review later. Thus, the emphasis must be on thinking through what you mean and how to verbalize it—what tone of voice you want to use, loud or soft, gentle or harsh, angry or calm, and so on.

Three key steps before verbally communicating are (1) consider what you want to say, (2) consider how you want to say it (e.g., parables may be more effective), and (3) consider the appropriate time to say it (timing can be critical, especially if the person is preoccupied when you attempt to deliver verbal communications).

At one point in my career, I used parable communication to make a point. I was vice president of marketing for a computer systems company when we discovered we had released a system with inadequate disk capacity to several major customers. I wanted to replace the disks with higher-capacity units free of charge, but the president was against this because of the cost we would incur. I was getting frustrated trying to get his support until I decided to use a parable to get my point across. Realizing the president was a Corvette fan and owned a brand-new Corvette, I asked him, "What would happen if General Motors discovered a design defect affecting your Corvette's performance?" He responded, "GM would recall the Corvette and fix the problem." I said, "And GM would have you pay for the recall, correct?" He said, "No, GM would pay for it." At that point, he realized the parallel to our disc problem and agreed to pay for the disc replacements.

Visual Communications Advice.

You may not write it or say it, but you still send visual signals either by the way you behave or by your body language. Like verbal communications, it can't be changed once expressed. This form is usually more revealing than written or verbal since it usually is an expression of your true feelings or emotions about a subject. Learning to control these subtle but obvious communiqués can become a real communications asset.

Additionally, one can use these visual forms of communications to amplify or even silently get a point across. For example, a cold stare can readily convey disapproval; fidgeting can convey a lack of interest or being uncomfortable about what is being said; a scowl can be interpreted as disapproval. On the positive side, a silent nod can convey agreement; a smile can convey amusement or agreement; maintaining eye contact can convey interest.

Chapter 39

Effective Communication Factors

Organize Your Thoughts.

Plan Your Delivery.

Analyze Results.

Communicating effectively goes a long way to achieving your goals. On the flip side, ineffective communication can be the biggest impediment to goal achievement. Therefore, it makes sense to take your communication skills seriously. The following three factors will provide you with more effective skills:

Organize Your Thoughts.

Organizing what you want to communicate is the beginning of effective communication. Too often we just open our mouths and start speaking, often resulting in a rambling dialogue leaving people scratching their heads. The first step in organizing your communication is to organize your thoughts. Ask yourself, "What do I want to have happen as a result of my communication?" Then develop a logical way to deliver the key points you wish to make. You may even want to rehearse your delivery ahead of time.

Plan Your Delivery.

The way in which you deliver your communication has a profound effect on the recipient's understanding. Some people receive written communication more readily, while others may be more receptive to visual or oral communication. Reflect on previous communications that were effective and determine what medium was used; try to tailor communication to that methodology. If the recipient has certain "hot buttons," try to use them to your advantage. For example, if the person is concerned about budget, point out the advantage of cost-saving features or revenue enhancements. Plan your timing for the communication. Pick a time when you can have the recipient's full attention without distraction.

Analyze Results.

Communication is not an isolated event that never repeats. It is a continual process, and therefore, today's communication results need to be taken into account for tomorrow's communication. Did your communication hold the recipient's attention? Did you make your key points in an effective, coherent manner? Were you understood? Did you achieve your desired result? Use this information to enhance your next communication.

Chapter 40

Key Meeting Elements

Establish Meeting Goals.

Establish Meeting Agenda.

Simplify Meeting Minutes.

Meetings range from being valuable management tools to being a total waste of time and money. Add up the hourly wages of meeting attendees, and you get a feel for what the meeting is costing the organization in out-of-pocket cost. If the meeting is ineffective, the opportunity cost (time wasted in an ineffective meeting and what could have been accomplished with that wasted time) can easily exceed the monetary loss. Three simple factors go a long way to ensure that meetings are effective:

Establish Meeting Goals.

What is the goal for the meeting (i.e., what will be accomplished during the meeting)? Clearly define the expected outcome ahead of time and publish this along with the meeting notice.

Establish Meeting Agenda.

Once the meeting goal has been established, develop an agenda that, when followed, will ensure that the meeting goal will be accomplished. List the agenda items sequentially, and publish the agenda along with the meeting goal in the meeting notice. One of my clients significantly reduced her meeting time by only attending meetings with a clearly defined goal and written agenda. Her motto was "no agenda, no meeting."

Simplify Meeting Minutes.

It is not necessary to document everything that happens in the meeting. The vital factors are the action items identified, who is responsible for each item, and when it will be accomplished. Use a form similar to the one shown here. This methodology clearly documents meeting results and provides documentation for tracking action items.

Action Item	Person Responsible	Completion Date

These three elements should be mandatory for every meeting you hold.

Chapter 41

Conducting Effective Meetings

Establish Meeting Goals and Agenda.

Have the Necessary Resources at the Meeting.

Establish Meeting Procedures.

In addition to having key meeting elements in place, you need to have an effective methodology for conducting meetings. The following three techniques have proven to effectively improve meeting efficiencies:

Establish Meeting Goals and Agenda.

Ahead of time, make sure a meeting goal or goals (end result) have been defined and an agenda developed to reach the meeting goal.

Have the Necessary Resources at the Meeting.

Meeting resources include getting the right people and information to the meeting, as well as the appropriate A/V equipment, flip charts, handouts, and so on. The key factor is getting the right people to the meeting, so check ahead of time and pick a time when the majority of key personnel can attend. If certain information will be necessary to achieve the meeting goal, make sure it is assembled and ready to go ahead of time.

Establish Meeting Procedures.

Beginning and ending on time is perhaps the most difficult element to achieve in conducting effective meetings. Establishing and communicating meeting procedures at the meeting's beginning significantly improves the odds of using meeting time efficiently and ending the meeting on time. These procedures can include the following strategies:

- Start on time (don't wait for stragglers; they will get the message soon enough that the meeting will begin without them).

- Set discussion time limits and use a timer to stick to them (too much discussion is just a rehash of what has already been said).

- Use a flip chart as a parking lot to document non-agenda items that arise (further discussion can take place after the main meeting agenda has been completed).

- Stick to the agenda (this should be obvious, but lots of meetings seem to wander all over the place).

- Allow personnel to leave the meeting once they have completed their contribution.

- In the meeting minutes document the key actions decided upon during the meeting, being sure to include the action item, who's responsible, and when it will be completed. After the meeting, distribute copies of the meeting minutes to meeting attendees.

These three simple elements contribute significantly to meeting effectiveness. Ask yourself, “Am I following these guidelines?” If not, there is room for improving your meeting effectiveness.

Chapter 42

Project Review Meeting Tips

Report Status.

Identify Corrective Actions.

Take Meeting Minutes.

Project review meetings usually involve all or at least a majority of project team members. Oftentimes, lengthy discussions take place that have little or no impact on other team members, thus wasting valuable time. To avoid this, follow these three simple meeting procedures:

Report Status.

Have each team member report the status of his or her project responsibility. Limit the status reports to either "on track" or "not on track." If on track, go to the next team member. If not on track, identify necessary corrective actions.

Identify Corrective Actions.

Have the not-on-track team member identify corrective action necessary to get back on track. If this involves other team members, have involved team members get together after the main meeting to discuss further actions and responsibilities.

Take Meeting Minutes.

The meeting minutes should only contain the three key factors from the meeting: (1) what will be done, (2) who is responsible, and (3) when it will be done. Document the meeting minutes on the following form for review at the next team meeting.

Action Item	Person Responsible	Completion Date

At the end of the meeting, provide each team member with a copy of the meeting minutes by Xerox copy or e-mail (see chapter 41, "Conducting Effective Meetings").

If everything is on track, the meeting will be very short. If not, this process guarantees the three critical issues for getting back on track will be addressed.

Chapter 43

Goal Alignment

Top-Level Goals.

Key Goal Action Items.

Supporting Goals.

An organization without goals is like a raft adrift on an open sea. An organization with unaligned goals is destined to failure. For success, it is essential that an organization not only have clearly stated goals, but that the goals throughout the organization are cascaded and clearly aligned. The following three items help ensure goal alignment in any organization:

Top-Level Goals.

Top-level goals identify the end results an organization will accomplish in any given time frame, usually annually. These top-level goals should be prioritized to avoid less important goals being accomplished at the expense of more vital goals.

I recommend that every organization identify three key goals that take precedence over lesser goals. This helps ensure the accomplishment of the most vital goals and provides direction to the organization as to where to first apply effort. An organization with ten top-level goals that are not prioritized will result in diluted effort among subordinate goals instead of focused effort on the most important subordinate goals.

Key Goal Action Items.

Once top-level goals have been determined and prioritized, identify the key action items that must be accomplished in order to achieve these top-level goals. By prioritizing the top-level goals, you automatically identify which action items are most vital for achieving high-priority goals. Once again, identify the top three action items for each of the top three goals. This results in nine key action items that must be accomplished. These nine action items then define subordinate goals. For example, if a top-level goal is to increase productivity by 5 percent, three key action items might be to (1) provide additional training to personnel, (2) reduce material shortage by 10 percent, and (3) redesign work flow.

Supporting Goals.

The three key action items to achieve top-level goals become subordinate goals for the organization. Thus, a subordinate goal becomes "To implement assembly techniques training for the production department by May 15." This goal, in turn, has three key action items, such as (1) complete training needs assessment by March 1, (2) select training program by April 1, and (3) develop training schedule by May 1. The process repeats itself as it cascades down into the organization.

The key concept here is to always identify the three most critical tasks that must be accomplished if the goals are to be achieved and to make sure they get done.

Chapter 44

Contingency Plan Guidelines

Identify the Three Most Likely Problems.

Don't Overplan Contingencies.

Act Decisively.

Planning is vital to obtaining results in any organization. Things don't just happen; they are made to happen by taking predetermined actions. The normal process is to develop a plan to achieve the desired results. However, expecting things to happen as planned is playing ostrich by putting your head in the sand, and it is just plain stupid. It ignores the fact that things rarely happen exactly as planned. Contingency plans will give you a head start on taking corrective action when things don't go as planned. Focus on the following three guidelines for contingency planning:

Identify the Three Most Likely Problems.

The key here is not to waste time trying to identify everything that might go wrong. The list is probably endless anyway, so why not focus on the three most likely problems to occur? It's okay to look at many things that might go wrong, but identify the three most likely, to limit the amount of unnecessary plans you and your team will have to develop.

Don't Overplan Contingencies.

While planning is one sure way to success, overplanning to deal with something that may never happen is a waste of valuable time. Simply identify the first three things that must be done if one of the three primary contingencies should occur. This gives you a head start on corrective actions when the contingency occurs, and simultaneously buys you time to figure out what the fourth, fifth, and sixth action steps will be.

Granted, the contingency that does occur may not be one of the three most likely that have been identified, but by identifying those top three, you are minimizing the odds that you will be unprepared when a contingency occurs.

Act Decisively.

When a contingency occurs, act decisively in taking predetermined corrective actions, and immediately identify further actions beyond the first three steps. Now that the contingency has actually occurred, you have specifics to deal with. You are no longer chasing elusive what-ifs. If the contingency is not one of the primary three previously identified, don't waste time wondering why you missed this particular contingency. Get busy identifying and assigning corrective actions.

Chapter 45

Discuss or Act?

Discuss during the Planning Stage.

***Act** during the Implementation Stage.*

Discuss and Modify during the Review Stage.

Discussion among team members is a good thing at the appropriate time, but can be disastrous at the wrong time. Imagine firefighters dealing with a major fire standing around discussing the best way to fight the fire instead of fighting the fire. Consider these three guidelines for discussing or acting:

Discuss during the Planning Stage.

My nephew commanded a lifeboat station on the Oregon coast and stated that the lifeboat crews spend much more time discussing, planning, and practicing rescue techniques than actually performing real rescue operations, due to the fact that emergency operations are not daily occurrences. As a result, the lifeboat crews follow previously developed best practices during rescue operations, saving valuable time and lives in the process.

In business, real-life operations are occurring daily, so managers and staff spend more time doing than planning. Nevertheless, planning is still essential, and certain periods of time are set aside to plan the year's operations, usually followed by quarterly plan update meetings. This is the time to discuss various techniques and plans. Debate the best way to accomplish results, be open to new ideas, listen to others, eliminate poor ideas, and so on. As the manager, you don't have to have the best ideas, but you do need to facilitate getting the best ideas from the planning process.

Act during the Implementation Stage.

Once the plan or procedures are in place, it is time to act. By this time, the team has already agreed on a course of action, and team members anticipate and expect planned performance from each other. If team members do not perform according to the agreed-upon plan, the plan falls apart. This does not mean that every action is dictated. Individuals use their best judgment when implementing plans and procedures, but they stay within the boundaries of the plan or procedure. If circumstances arise that obsolete the plan, contingency plans come into play, and new plans are established.

Discuss and Modify during the Review Stage.

In my nephew's rescue operations, the crews hold a postincident review to assess what went right, what went wrong, and what could have been done better. This same procedure is also routinely followed by fire departments after each incident.

As business teams move forward, it often becomes necessary to modify plans or procedures. Discuss what is working, what is not working, and what can be improved upon. Proceeding when the plan or procedure is not working is folly. If things change, the team obviously changes the plan or procedure to adapt or take advantage of better ideas. This is an iterative process, eventually leading to best practices.

Chapter 46

Effective Change Management

Assess What Needs Changing.

Clearly Define and Communicate Change.

Involve People in Change.

As managers, we initiate change or we fall behind. Imagine a company that never improves or changes its product line. That company will fall by the wayside in no time at all. The old adage "The only thing that doesn't change is change itself" is as true today as it was yesterday, and it will be equally true forever. Managing change successfully involves three key elements:

Assess What Needs Changing.

The first step in any change is determining what needs changing. It is critical to keep an open mind during this phase of the change process. A good tool to identify the need for change is the use of a SWOT (strengths, weaknesses, opportunities, and threats) chart. Once these four factors are identified, use strengths to overcome weaknesses, realize opportunities, and eliminate threats.

In addition, listen to others and seek their opinion on what needs changing, and assess the benefits of proposed change versus the effort required to implement the change. George Washington strongly believed in soliciting and listening to others' inputs based on the premise that doing so gave him more options than relying solely on his own knowledge.

Clearly Define and Communicate Change.

Once needed change has been identified, make sure it is clearly defined and communicated, especially to those who will be involved in effecting the change. Don't overlook explaining why the change is needed and the benefits associated with the change. The better change is understood, the better equipped your organization will be to effect the change.

Involve People in Change.

People have a natural tendency to resist change. By involving team members in identifying needed or desired change and how to effect that change, you are in effect transferring ownership of the change process to the team. The worst scenario would be for team members to be asked to change when the way to implement change has been dictated to them without their input. Team ownership of the change process is essential to success, and as the manager, your major focus should be to ensure that the team is embracing change.

While these three steps are simply common sense, it is amazing how many managers rush headlong into change without asking themselves three questions:

> Have I accurately assessed the need for change?
>
> Have I clearly defined and communicated the need for change?

> Have I involved my team members in how the change will be implemented?

Answering yes to these three questions puts you on the right track to successfully implement change.

Chapter 47

Effective To-Do Lists

Align with Goals.

Prioritize according to Goals.

Check Feasibility.

Everyone is familiar with to-do lists, but is a to-do list really effective? The answer is yes, no, or maybe. If your list contains too many items, the likelihood of getting everything done is slim, and the list carries over from day to day, eventually becoming a daily albatross. Your list doesn't have to only contain tasks that you personally must do. Items to be delegated should also be considered. To be really effective, your to-do list must contain three things:

Align with Goals.

The items on your list must relate to making progress toward your goals. There are lots of things a manager needs to do, but maintaining focus on goal progress is vital. At the end of the day, it doesn't make any difference how many things you accomplished if you haven't made progress toward your goals.

Prioritize according to Goals.

Prioritize the tasks on your list according to importance. Differentiate between vital and urgent tasks. Take into account the time frame involved. Some tasks may be vital but not urgent, while others may be less vital but more urgent, therefore having a higher priority. List your tasks as A, B, or C priority, and do the A tasks first. Don't make every task an A priority. If two tasks have the same level of importance, designate them as A-1 and A-2, and do A-1 first.

Check Feasibility.

Can the task be performed today? If it can't be completed today, the task should be broken down into sequential subtasks that can be accomplished in one day. Follow-on sequential tasks are then scheduled for following days. Nothing is more frustrating than having to carry over tasks on your to-do list day after day, and nothing is more rewarding than crossing everything off your list on a daily basis. If you find your list encompasses too many items, consider delegating some of the tasks.

Chapter 48

Key Time Management Factors

Analyze Current Time Usage.

Align Time with Your Vital Few.

Eliminate Time Wasters.

Effective time management goes a long way in improving your personal efficiency. The following three factors are key to attaining effective time management and need to be repeated on a regular basis to maintain highest efficiency:

Analyze Current Time Usage.

Demands for our time as managers are dynamic, to say the least. Some of the demands are vital, some urgent, and a few are vital and urgent. It's a good idea, on a quarterly basis, to analyze how you are spending your time. Review your schedule daily and keep a time usage log, to factually determine where your time is being spent. This formal process of logging your time usage is essential in today's hectic management environment, since it is often difficult at the end of the day to remember all the demands that were placed on your time.

Align Time with Your Vital Few.

Once you have determined your current time usage, compare that usage to your vital few (i.e., those tasks that are vital to achieving your goals, either personal or professional). The ground rule here demands that your time is used first to accomplish tasks leading to goal attainment.

Differentiate between what is vital and what is urgent. What is urgent is not always vital, and what is vital is not always urgent. In fact, most vital tasks start out as vital and nonurgent, but with the passage of time and various distractions, these vital, nonurgent factors will have a tendency to migrate to the vital-urgent quadrant. The way to eliminate this risk is to regularly spend time on the vital-nonurgent items. Review your time usage log daily and identify activities that do not move you closer to attaining your vital goals, and either eliminate them or at least minimize them.

After analyzing my time usage, I discovered that my personal productivity varied during the day, with my most productive time occurring between 8:30 a.m. and 9:30 a.m., before getting embroiled in the daily activities. This gave me time to have a cup of coffee and review the status of the current vital factors before rolling up my sleeves. Once I discovered this, I designated this as my "*power hour*" and arranged my schedule to leave the hour free to address the *vital few*. I communicated this to my staff and asked them to see me outside my power hour to minimize my power-hour interruptions. Simultaneously I encouraged them to define and synchronize their own power hours.

Eliminate Time Wasters.

Unfortunately, not every activity we engage in is a productive use of our time. In other words, the activity does not address our vital few, and therefore is an ineffective use of precious time. Study the next chapter, "Time Wasters," to help identify time wasters and possible solutions.

Chapter 49

Time Wasters

Possible Time Waster	Possible Solutions
Telephone interruptions	Use voice mail effectively, and set aside specific time to return calls.
Drop-in visitors	Take control and put it on your terms … "I'm really busy right now; let me get back to you." Use do-not-disturb indicators.
Staff interruptions	Schedule time for interruptions; Schedule time for staff one-on-ones.
Requests for assistance	Don't be afraid to say, "I'm busy right now; can we do this later?" Do your work first.
Accepting others' monkeys	Use the monkey mirror.

Micromanaging	Clearly define expected results and review cycles; Focus on results, not details.
Being too social	Be nice, but be brief.
Unplanned day	Set a daily plan and prioritized to-do lists.
Working on non-vital tasks	Delegate and prioritize.
Changing priorities	Seek clarification on priority.
Junk mail	Toss it promptly.
E-mail spam	Don't open if sender is not recognized; Set filters.
Internet distractions	Complete work before playing.
Overly tired and low efficiency	Take short breaks.
Large pending file	Don't procrastinate; Handle paper once.
Meetings	Insist on meeting goal and agenda; Start and end on time; Use the parking lot.
Analysis paralysis	Trust first impressions.

Chapter 50

Coping with Change

Expect Change.

Understand Change.

Don't Overreact.

The axiom "Change is constant" is as true today as it was at the beginning of time. As managers, we must deal with change on a daily basis, whether it is an employee who doesn't show up for work or a project hitting a snag. Change can be frustrating and create enormous stress in the manager as well as employees, especially when we don't put change into perspective. The following three tips will help managers take change in stride:

Expect Change.

Change is all around us; it happens on both a regular and irregular basis, and we can't always predict it. But we can expect it and realize it is a part of our managerial life. We get paid to deal with change, so the sooner we recognize that dealing with change is an unwritten part of our job description, the sooner we can learn to take it in stride. Managers who get rattled when change occurs create stress and concern among their staff. Managers who take change in stride provide calm leadership to those around them.

Understand Change.

When change occurs, it is essential to understand why the change occurred. Was it expected or unexpected? If expected, were you ready for it? If unexpected, could it have been anticipated? The answers to these three questions provide a basis for dealing with future change. If change is expected, you have the opportunity to develop plans for dealing with it. Don't ignore expected change, or you will be at its mercy. You can also have a system for dealing with unexpected change. This will give you a head start in dealing with unexpected change in a calm, rational manner.

Don't Overreact.

When expected change occurs, invoke your plan for dealing with it. Having a plan allows you to deal with it in a calm, unemotional, logical manner. For unexpected change, invoke your system for dealing with unexpected change. Once again, this will allow you to deal with it in a calm, unemotional, logical manner.

If you find yourself in a situation where you lack a plan to deal with expected change or don't have a system for managing unexpected change, don't panic or overreact. Remaining calm fosters rational thinking, so you can identify what can be done about it and develop an action plan for dealing with the change.

Chapter 51

Key Interviewing Techniques

Be Prepared.

Check Past Performance.

Do a Postinterview Assessment.

Understanding interviewing techniques is extremely important; having good interviewing techniques is perhaps one of the most important management skills a person may possess. Getting it wrong leaves you with two major problems: (1) the person you hire doesn't do the job properly, and (2) you have to correct the hiring mistake.

Common mistakes in the interviewing process include hiring in your own image, being overly impressed by an applicant's demeanor, wasting time during the interview, hiring based on gut feeling while ignoring data, being overly impressed by credentials, and succumbing to pressure to fill the job.

Understanding the following three key interviewing techniques will help you hire the right person the first time, reduce time dealing with poor performance, and strengthen the team with each new hire.

Be Prepared.

Understand the requirements of the position to be filled and assess potential candidates' qualifications against those requirements. Determine the key performance criteria for the position to be filled and identify the candidate's key skills that relate to those criteria. Assemble an interviewing team and hold a preinterview meeting to determine what information each team member will seek, thus avoiding redundancy in the interview.

Check Past Performance.

The best predictor of future performance is past performance, so zero in on exactly what the candidate's actual past performance was. What specific part did the person play in past key events? What specific results did the candidate achieve in these key events? Was he or she merely a member of the team that accomplished significant results, or did the candidate actually accomplish or direct the results himself or herself?

Practice good listening skills during the interview. Don't monopolize the conversation. Use silence effectively to let the candidate talk. Be sure to check the candidate's references against the claims made in the interview (e.g., "I understand the candidate worked on project ABC. What were his or her contributions to that project?").

Do a Postinterview Assessment.

Hold a postinterview meeting with the interviewing team to determine the overall knowledge, expertise, and experience the candidate actually possesses. What one misses, another will likely catch. The meeting will also help identify any inconsistency in the candidate's responses, as well as identifying how well the candidate might fit into the existing team. Look for unanimous agreement among the interviewing team. If an offer is to be made without unanimous agreement, clearly understand the validity for doing so.

Chapter 52

Effort vs. Reward

What Effort Is Required?

What Is the Reward?

Is the Reward Worth the Effort?

The old saying "There's always room for improvement" is as true today as it was yesterday and as true as it will be tomorrow. But making improvement requires effort in addition to the effort currently being expended. And where do we find the time to make these improvement changes? The following three things should be considered before embarking on change for improvement:

What Effort Is Required?

In the ideal world, the team's effort is 100 percent utilized to achieve goals. If this is the case, one might question whether the team has the capacity to exert additional effort to realize change. In the real world, the team's effort utilization is usually somewhere between 80 percent and 120 percent. In this range, there is effort that can be expended to realize change necessary to achieve desired improved performance. Going beyond the 100 percent level for extended periods of time will stretch the team's capability and can result in burnout. The closer the level is to 120 percent, the faster burnout becomes a reality.

So the key question is, "Is stretching the team worth the results achieved?" Results achieved must include the negative factors as well as the positive factors, such as the effect on the team's morale, personal lives, burnout, and so on.

What Is the Reward?

Before invoking change, clearly identify the expected benefits, as well as the ramifications of the increased effort. Will it make a significant or marginal improvement? Marginal improvements should only require a marginal increase in effort for a short period of time. Significant effort for marginal improvement is obviously not worthwhile. The ideal is significant improvement for marginal effort.

Is the Reward Worth the Effort?

Any change requires the exertion of effort above and beyond current levels. However, the additional effort should be finite and time-limited, while the improvement should be ongoing once improvements have been achieved and are in place.

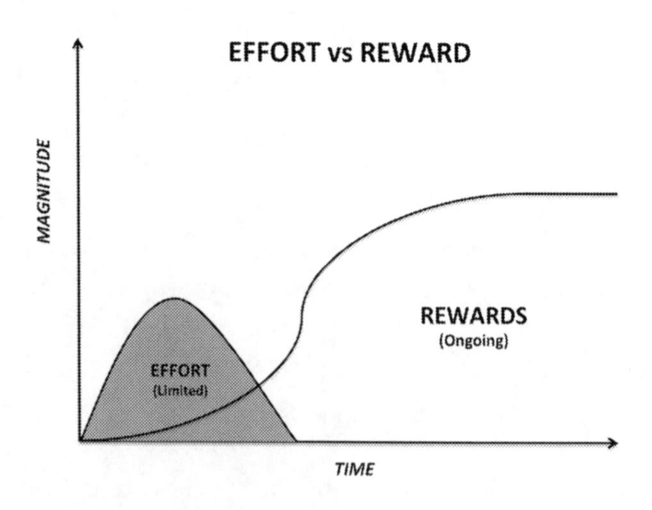

Endnotes

1. **Vilfredo Pareto** (1848–1923) was an Italian economist who, in 1906, observed that 20 percent of the Italian people owned 80 percent of their country's accumulated wealth. http://www.bsu.edu/libraries/ahafner/awh-th-math-pareto.html.

2. "In recent months, Microsoft has learned that 80 percent of the errors and crashes in Windows and Office are caused by 20 percent of the entire pool of bugs detected and that more than 50 percent of the headaches derive from a mere 1 percent of all flawed code." By Paula Rooney in the October 3, 2002, issue of CRN. http://www.crn.com/news/%20security/18821726/microsofts-ceo-80-20-rule-applies-to-bugs-not-just-features.htm.

3. A chart that gave the inequality a very visible and comprehensible form, the so-called "champagne glass" effect, was contained in the 1992 United Nations Development Program Report, which showed the distribution of global income to be very uneven, with the richest 20 percent of the world's population controlling 82.7 percent of the world's income. http://hdr.undp.org/en/media/hdr_1992_en_chap3.pdf.

About the Author

Dr. Hill has achieved success both academically and professionally. After enlisting in the US Coast Guard, he was one of three (out of over fifty) recruits selected to attend electronics technician school, where he finished first in his class. During his four-year Coast Guard enlistment, he advanced six ranks, from seaman recruit to first-class electronics technician.

Upon completion of his Coast Guard enlistment, Dr. Hill obtained magna and summa cum laude degrees in electrical engineering (bachelor and master of science), a PhD in engineering science (specializing in surface physics), and an MBA. His MBA was obtained from the University of Portland in one year with a 4.0 grade point average while working full-time.

During his professional career, Dr. Hill has worked as a design engineer, manager of software development, product marketing manager, VP engineering, VP corporate development, VP European operations, VP worldwide sales and marketing, president and CEO of public and private companies, and founder, president, and CEO of a successful management consulting firm with several hundred clients over a twelve-year period.